POLAND'S JEWISH LANDMARKS

A Travel Guide

POLAND'S JEWISH LANDMARKS

A Travel Guide

JORAM KAGAN

HIPPOCRENE BOOKS, INC.
New York

ISBN 0-7818-0851-0

For information, address:
HIPPOCRENE BOOKS, INC.
171 Madison Avenue
New York, NY 10016
www.hippocrenebooks.com

Cataloging-in-Publication Data available from the Library of Congress.

Printed in the United States of America.

To the Righteous Few

Contents

Acknowledgments

I wish to express my gratitude to Akiva Kohane and Paula Borenstein for my initial introduction to "Jewish" Poland; to Monika Krajewska and Malgorzata Niezabitowska, whose work on Polish Jewry has left a lasting impression on me; and to my friends, Marian Turski and Jerzy Tomaszewski, who have no peers in the knowledge of Polish-Jewish history.

My special thanks go to Dr. Simha Wajs for his unique efforts to commemorate the Jewry of Lublin, my hometown.

It was always a pleasure to see Mordechai Palzur—a friend whose hospitality was matchless while he served as Israel's ambassador to Poland.

I also wish to acknowledge the assistance given to me during my thirty trips to Poland by the people of Lot Polish Airlines.

I greatly appreciate the generous permission of Henryk Grynberg to quote his magnificent poem, "Poplars." Martin Gilbert's permission to reproduce his world-famous maps enabled me to add historical perspective to this work. I am confident that his kindness and skill will make all the difference to the reader.

Last but not least, I thank Marion Donnal and Sabina Franco for "suffering in silence" through my numerous changes and additions to the manuscript, as well as Rafi Rothstein, Sylvia Bruzzese, and Daphna Raz, whose encouragement was always most welcome.

There are, of course, many more individuals whom I met during my frequent trips to Poland, and who always added some new dimension to my knowledge. They are too numerous to be mentioned by name, unfortunately, but I thank them all.

Preface

By and large, both English and Polish nomenclatures are used to identify cities and towns in this guide—Warsaw *(Warszawa)*, Cracow *(Krakow)*, etc. Shtetl names are also present in certain instances, as these were widely used by Jewish immigrants to the United States. Thus Tykocin appears as Tiktin, for example.

In order to facilitate the location of sites, Polish designations are utilized: *Ulica* = Street; *Aleje* = Avenue; *Plac* = Square. Beyond these general concepts, however, the issue becomes more complicated. For upon the restoration of Poland's sovereignty in 1989, Poles began to rename the streets, squares, and avenues that honored former communist leaders. Since this renaming process is ongoing, a few of the addresses given in the book may be outdated. That being said, the actual physical locations of the sites—buildings, synagogues, monuments, cemeteries, etc.—remain unchanged.

Names of persons may assume the Polish or English spelling—Sztajn versus Shtein/Stein, being one example—depending on the source(s) of information.

Some Hebrew words are used when they describe the subject more accurately, such as *Beth Midrash* (Institute of Learning); *Matzevot* (tombstones); *Minyan* (ten adult Jewish males required for communal worship); *Ohel* (tent grave); *Shoah* (Holocaust); and *Tzadik* (righteous person).

Typography

Due to typographic limitations, some typical Polish letters are represented by their English approximates in the following fashion:

ą = a
ć = c
ę = e
ł = l
ń = n
ó = o
ś = s
ż = z
ź = z

One Additional Note

Unless otherwise stated in the text, “war” refers to World War II.

MOURNER'S KADDISH

Yitgadal v'yitkadash sh'mei raba b'alma di v'ra chirutei, v'yamlich malchutei b'cha-yeichon uv-yomeichon, uv-cha-yei d'chol bet Yisrael, ba'agala u-vizman kariv, v'imru Amein.

יִתְגַּדַּל וְיִתְקַדַּשׁ שְׁמֵהּ רַבָּא
בְּעָלְמָא דִּי בְרָא כִרְעוּתֵהּ,
וְיַמְלִיךְ מַלְכוּתֵהּ, בְּחַיֵּיכוֹן
וּבְיוֹמֵיכוֹן, וּבְחַיֵּי דְכָל־בֵּית
יִשְׂרָאֵל, בַּעֲגָלָא וּבִזְמַן קָרִיב,
וְאִמְרוּ אָמֵן.

Y'hei sh'mei raba m'vorach l'alam ul-almei almaya.

יְהֵא שְׁמֵהּ רַבָּא מְבָרַךְ לְעָלַם
וּלְעָלְמֵי עָלְמַיָּא.

Yitbarach v'yishtabach v'yitpa'ar v'yitromam v'yitnasei, v'yit-hadar v'yitaleh v'yit-halal sh'mei d'kudsha, b'rich Hu. L'eilah (l'eilah) min kol birchata v'shirata, tushb'chata v'nechemata, da'amiran b'alma, v'imru Amein.

יִתְבָּרַךְ וְיִשְׁתַּבַּח וְיִתְפָּאַר
וְיִתְרוֹמַם וְיִתְנַשֵּׂא, וְיִתְהַדַּר
וְיִתְעַלֶּה וְיִתְהַלָּל שְׁמֵהּ
דְּקֻדְשָׁא, בְּרִיךְ הוּא. לְעֵלָּא
(לְעֵלָּא) מִן כָּל־בִּרְכָתָא
וְשִׁירָתָא, תֻּשְׁבְּחָתָא וְנֶחֱמָתָא,
דַּאֲמִירָן בְּעָלְמָא, וְאִמְרוּ אָמֵן.

Y'hei sh'lama raba min sh'maya, v'chayim aleinu v'al kol Yisrael, v'imru Amein.

יְהֵא שְׁלָמָא רַבָּא מִן שְׁמַיָּא,
וְחַיִּים עָלֵינוּ וְעַל כָּל־יִשְׂרָאֵל,
וְאִמְרוּ אָמֵן.

POPLARS

by Henryk Grynberg

They stand in a row like chimneys,
sooty Italian poplars
signposts to heaven
tall
like the local silence
they grew here all the time
in spite of
and above all
and they're still growing

while the air here is thick
with absence
clouds of absence in the air
and an emptiness called forgetting
ascends to heaven like a cloud

trodden by feet in the millions
the great Auschwitz field
the Auschwitz field of Maidanek
the Auschwitz field of Treblinka
the Auschwitz field of All This

on which we stand
move with us
wherever we try to go
so one can't get anyplace from here
nor leave here

I halt in the row of poplars
and try to grow along with them
and like them to gaze
upwards
with green eyes
I don't try to understand anything
nor say anything
what else can one
have to say here

I come here to add my own
to the growing silence

CHAPTER 1

Chronology of Jewish Presence in Poland Before and After WWII

A.D.

860 Jewish merchant, Ibn Kordabeh of Spain, visits Poland.

960 Ibrahim Ibn Jakob, a Jewish traveler from Spanish Toledo, writes an extensive account of Poland entitled *Mieszko's Land*—the first historical mention of the country.

1018 Due to persecution, Jews migrate to Poland from Bohemia.

1096 A wave of Jewish settlers arrives from Western Europe in the wake of the First Crusade.

1147 Another wave of Jews migrates in response to persecution aggravated by the activities of the Second Crusade.

1264 Prince Boleslaw the Pious issues the *Statute of Kalisz* writ, which establishes and protects the legal position of Jews in Poland.

1267 Polish Church Council of Wroclaw (Breslau) outlines its anti-Jewish policies, seeking to segregate Jews from Christians.

1283 First Jewish cemetery is established in the town of Kalisz.

1334 King Casimir III the Great (Kazimierz Wielki) broadens and ratifies the *Statute of Kalisz*.

1399	First case of "ritual murder" enters the courts, marking the beginning of renewed Jewish persecution.
1453	King Casimir IV Jagiello codifies the legal status of Jews. He entrusts salt mines and customs stations to Jewish managers.
1483	Expulsion of Jews from Warsaw, subsequently rescinded.
1495	Expulsion of Jews from Lithuania (then part of the Polish Union).
1495	Settlement of Cracow Jews in Kazimierz.
1503	Readmission of Jews into Lithuania.
1503	Rabbi Jacob Polak appointed the "Rabbi of Poland."
1507	King Sigismund I the Elder reconfirms Jewish privilege.
1527	Warsaw introduces *Privilegia De Non Tolerantis Judaeis* under Sigismund I.
1534	Sigismund I decrees that Jews need not wear a distinguishing mark upon their clothing.
1534	First Hebrew printing press established in Cracow.
1572	Death of Moshe Ben Israel Iserless (Remu).
1576	King Steven Batory outlaws accusations of ritual murder.
1579	Jewish Sejm (Parliament) convenes.
1581–1764	Period of Jewish Autonomy—Sejm of Four Lands.
1648–1649	Jews of eastern Poland are ravaged by Chmielnicki, the Ukrainian Cossack nationalist revolt and massacres, Tartar incursions from Crimea, and the Swedish War.
1712	Jews expelled from Sandomierz, subsequently rescinded.

1755	Jacob Frank starts the Frankist Movement.
1760	Death of Baal Shem Tov (Hassidic Movement).
1764	Census in Poland-Lithuania counts 749,968 Jews.
1771	Eliahu Goan of Vilna (Wilno) passes first curse on Hassidim.
1772	Enlightened Polish leaders—H. Kollataj and T. Czacki, for example—attempt to improve legal and social status of Jews.
1791	Death of Jacob Frank; Constitution of May Third.
1794	Colonel Berek Joselewicz leads the Jewish Legion in Kosciuszko's Uprising against the Russians.
1797	Death of Gaon of Vilna—head of the Mitnagdim Movement opposing Hassidism.
1807	Constitution of the Duchy of Warsaw grants Jews equality.
1815	1,657 Polish Jews participate in the Leipzig Fair.
1891	Imperial Russia's anti-Semitic May Laws are introduced into Poland, then a Russian province (until 1918).
1908	Bund is founded.
1916	School quotas are imposed with the result that many Jews are expelled from educational establishments.
1916	Agudat Israel is founded.
1918	Poland regains its independence.
1922	General Zionist Party emerges as the dominant voice and political force of Polish Jewry.
1925	YIVO, the Institute for Jewish Studies is founded in Vilna (Wilno).
1930	Yeshivat Hachamei Lublin is founded.

Chronology of World War II events found in Warsaw Ghetto Timeline (page 199).

1945	2,982,000 Polish Jews are killed during the course of the war, meaning that only approximately 55,500 survive.
1946	Pogroms in Cracow and Kielce.
1947	Jewish Historical Institute *(Zydowski Instytut Historyczny)* is established.
1948	Poland recognizes Israel. A diplomatic legation ensues.
1949	Jewish Religious Organization is established in Poland.
1950	End of first mass emigration that further depletes Polish Jewry.
1955	Jewish (Yiddish) State Theater is founded under Ida Kaminska.
1956	American Jewish Distribution Committee (JOINT) renews operations in Poland.
1958	50,000 Polish Jews emigrate from Poland.
1963	Israeli Mission to Poland is elevated to the status of an embassy.
1967	In step with the Soviet Union, the Polish government breaks off all diplomatic relations with Israel following the Six-Day War.
1968	On the heels of government-sponsored anti-Semitism, a fourth mass emigration of Polish Jews occurs.
1981	After an interruption, the American Joint Distribution Committee resumes its activities in Poland.
1986	Israel Interest Section established in Warsaw under Ambassador Mordechai Palzur.

1987 El Al Airlines and Lot Polish Airlines inaugurate Warsaw-Tel Aviv service.

1990 On February 27, full diplomatic relations with Israel are reestablished at an ambassadorial level.

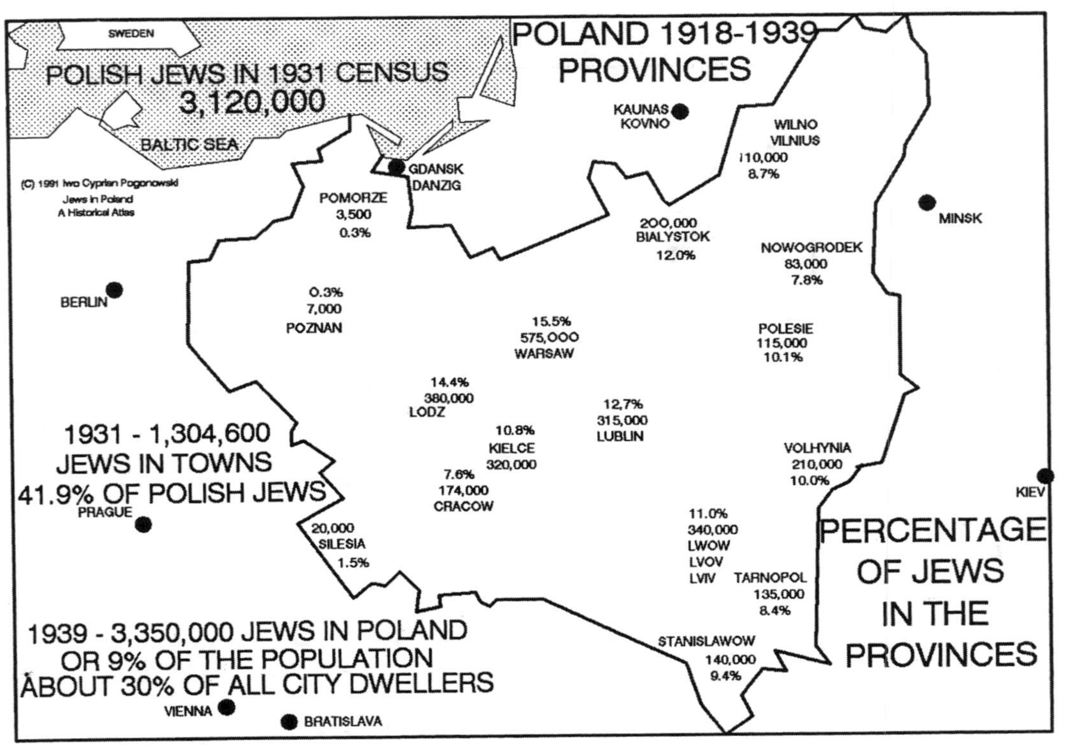
SWEDEN
POLISH JEWS IN 1931 CENSUS
3,120,000
BALTIC SEA
POLAND 1918-1939
PROVINCES
(C) 1991 Iwo Cyprian Pogonowski
Jews in Poland
A Historical Atlas
KAUNAS
KOVNO
GDANSK
DANZIG
WILNO
VILNIUS
110,000
8.7%
MINSK
POMORZE
3,500
0.3%
200,000
BIALYSTOK
12.0%
NOWOGRODEK
83,000
7.8%
BERLIN
0.3%
7,000
POZNAN
15.5%
575,000
WARSAW
POLESIE
115,000
10.1%
14.4%
380,000
LODZ
12,7%
315,000
LUBLIN
10.8%
KIELCE
320,000
VOLHYNIA
210,000
10.0%
1931 - 1,304,600
JEWS IN TOWNS
41.9% OF POLISH JEWS
PRAGUE
7.6%
174,000
CRACOW
KIEV
20,000
SILESIA
1.5%
11.0%
340,000
LWOW
LVOV
LVIV
TARNOPOL
135,000
8.4%
PERCENTAGE
OF JEWS
IN THE
PROVINCES
STANISLAWOW
140,000
9.4%
1939 - 3,350,000 JEWS IN POLAND
OR 9% OF THE POPULATION
ABOUT 30% OF ALL CITY DWELLERS
VIENNA
BRATISLAVA

Jews in the Provinces—1931.

CHAPTER 2

Introduction to Polish Jewry Culture

A CONCISE HISTORY

Before the Second World War, the Jewish community of Poland was the largest such community in Europe and the second largest in the entire world. It numbered 3.1 million members according to the 1931 census, or approximately 10% of the country's total population. This percentage was even greater in cities, reaching 33% in Warsaw—or more than the entire Jewry of France—75% in Pinsk, and 51% in Bialystok.

Ibrahim Ibn Jakob, a Jewish traveler from Spain, authored the first written document about Poland. In the account of his journey from 960–965, he writes, among other things, about "Mieszko's Land." There is a legend that ascribes the first Jewish settlement in Poland to a heavenly command for wandering Jews to "Polin" ("Rest here"). Some consider it a pun, however, and attribute it to Rabbi Moshe Iserless of Cracow (Remu).

The first Jewish settlers in Poland arrived in the seventh to ninth centuries; though more numerous waves immigrated between the twelfth and fifteenth centuries, when the countries of Western Europe persecuted and banished Jews in the wake of Crusades and other wars. Jews found protection and tolerance in Poland, a country in need of enterprising merchants and craftsmen. As such, they obtained "privileges" from Duke Boleslaw the Pious in 1264, and from King Casimir the Great 100 years later. Legend has it that these latter privileges were granted, in some measure, due to Casimir's love for a Jewish girl named Esther (Esterka); furthermore, it is said that the sons of this liaison were raised as Christians and the daughters as Jews.

There were also practical reasons to welcome Jews after the Mongol invasion that had left vast territories depopulated. The Jews, for their part, were eager to move east, driven by insecurity and fear in the face of the Crusades and massacres in German-Moravian-Bohemian towns.

The Jews of the time were engaged in a variety of trades and crafts, as well as in banking and tax collecting. They took inns, mills, and distilleries on lease, and participated in other areas of economic life including agriculture. In international trade, they provided important links with the Moslem world.

The fourteenth century saw the establishment of Jewish communities in Lwow, Sandomierz, Poznan, Brzesc, and Troki. Upon Poland's unification, King Casimir (Kazimierz Wielki) ratified and broadened the "privileges" statute in 1334, 1364, and 1367. Included in these acts were provisions that protected money lending as an occupation.

At the same time, the Jewish presence was marred by massacres during the Black Death and the official anti-Jewish policy initiated in Wroclaw (Breslau) by the Church Council of 1267. Despite these hardships, there would be as many as 30,000 Jews in Poland by the end of the fifteenth century.

In Lithuania, a part of the Polish Union in which the Jews were originally welcomed, they were expelled in 1495 and then readmitted in 1503. Various forms of

Jewish autonomy existed—the best known being the Council of Four Lands (*Va'ad Arbaa Aratzoth*)—despite the persistently ambiguous legal position of Jews. This would continue to be the case throughout the sixteenth and seventeenth centuries, when Jewish autonomy was reaffirmed by various Polish leaders, even as it was being undermined by various decrees of *Privilegia De Non-Tolerantis Judaeis*.

The Chmielnicki's Ukrainian revolt and subsequent wars with Moscow and Sweden decimated the Jewish community; once again, however, it rebounded to reach 750,000 at the time of the 1764 census.

By the latter part of the eighteenth century, the Jewish population had been partitioned—as Poland itself had been—among Austria, Germany, and Russia. This new situation deeply affected the structure of the Jewish community. Many enlightened Polish leaders, such as Kollataj and Czacki, promoted Jewish emancipation; while Staszyc and Czartoryski demanded the end of the "Jewish State within the State."

At the same time, Poland began to emerge as a powerful center of Jewish culture. The Jewish population included both the Ashkenazim and Sephardim, who had fled or were expelled from Spain and Portugal in the fifteenth century. This cultural differentiation of the Jewish community bred a specific type of Polish Jew, and led to clashes among various religious and cultural currents that would continue to rage on into the following century. Throughout it all, most Jews chose to hold fast to their religious and cultural customs, and to preserve their identity; others aspired to join Polish society, frequently at the cost of their religious faith.

The middle of the nineteenth century witnessed the Kronenberg, Natanson, Epstein, Wawelberg, Rotwant,

Toeplitz, Reichman, and Bloch families develop and organize many facets of Poland's economic and cultural life. They were pioneers in the country's modern banking system and industry, as well as in engineering, the paper trade, and transport—Vistula River navigation and railway lines linking Warsaw with Vienna, for example. Polish Jews also initiated the development of the phonographic and film industries, and nurtured the Polish press and book publishing.

In addition to such renowned Yiddish writers as Icchak Perec, Shalom Asch, and Shalom Aleichem, Jews also made lasting contributions to Polish-language literature, arts, and music. Nineteenth-century directors of the Warsaw Opera House, for example, included Adam Munchheimer and Ludwik Grossman; while the co-founder and builder of the Warsaw Philharmonic Hall, opened in 1901, was Alexander Reichman.

Jews had taken part in the Polish national liberation movements and uprisings of 1794, 1830–1831, and 1863; so, too, would they fight in the revolt of 1905, the battles against Poland's occupiers in WWI, and the struggles for independence in 1918.

The resulting post-war Polish Republic was a country of minorities such as Jews, Byelorussians, Ukrainians, and Germans—all of whom were protected by the Treaty of Versailles. The Polish minorities' treaty went even further, stipulating provisions for Jewish schools and respect for the Shabbat. In practice, however, these provisions failed: the use of Hebrew and Yiddish was discouraged, and *numerus clausus* (school quotas) restricted Jewish education in high schools and universities.

The economic situation of the Jews deteriorated in the 1930s, forcing many members of the community to rely on foreign aid. This downturn also fostered the growth of the Zionist movement, which included Hehalutz, Hehalutz Hatzair, Hashomer Hatzair, General Zionist, and Labor Zionist groups.

Despite these economic and political pressures, the situation of Jews in Poland was bearable during the rule of Marshal Pilsudski. After his death in 1935 and the rise of his successors, however, it quickly worsened.

In response, the Jewish population of Poland developed numerous political parties, including Bund, Poalei Zion, and the Communists on the left; the centrist Folkists; the right-wing General Zionists; and Orthodox Jewish groups such as Mizrahi and Aguda. There were also strong Jewish trade unions and groups aspiring to assimilation within the larger Polish community. Jews had representatives in both chambers of the Polish parliament and in many local town councils.

Jews of the time continued to be active in trade, crafts, and industry, as well as in the legal, medical, and many other professions. Some worked as agents of large and primarily absentee landowners—an occupation that gave rise to anti-Semitism in no small measure. As a whole, Jews played an outstanding role in the development of towns and industry. Despite the influence of foreign capital in Lodz, for example, the textile industry was primarily in the hands of prominent families such as the Wislickis, Poznanskis, Kohns, and Ettingers. The most active Jewish industrial and cultural centers were Warsaw, Cracow, Lodz, Lublin, Bialystok, Zamosc, Kalisz, and until WWII, Lvov (Lwow) and Polish Vilna (Wilno).

Jews also made significant contributions to the creation of urban housing and other residential facilities. They built their own public buildings, schools and theaters, synagogues, cemeteries, hospitals, and orphanages.

In addition, the Jewish communities in larger cities constructed unique museums, archives, and libraries (see Chapter 5).

The outbreak of WWII brought devastation to Poland's Jewish community and their urban centers. During the September campaign of 1939 alone, when Germany ruthlessly invaded Poland, 30% of all Jewish-affiliated buildings were destroyed. Twenty thousand Jewish civilians were killed, in addition to 32,216 officers and soldiers. Another 61,000 became POWs, of whom very few ultimately survived. Synagogue burnings, humiliations, and arrests subsequently became everyday events. By 1944, Poland would become the largest Jewish cemetery in the world. The struggle and martyrdom of Polish Jewry will be described in different parts of this book.

SECOND WORLD WAR

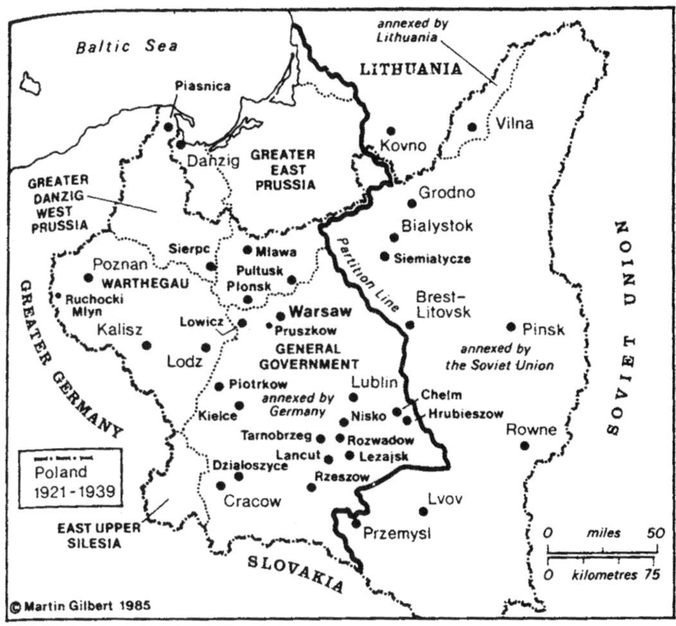

Courtesy of Martin Gilbert.

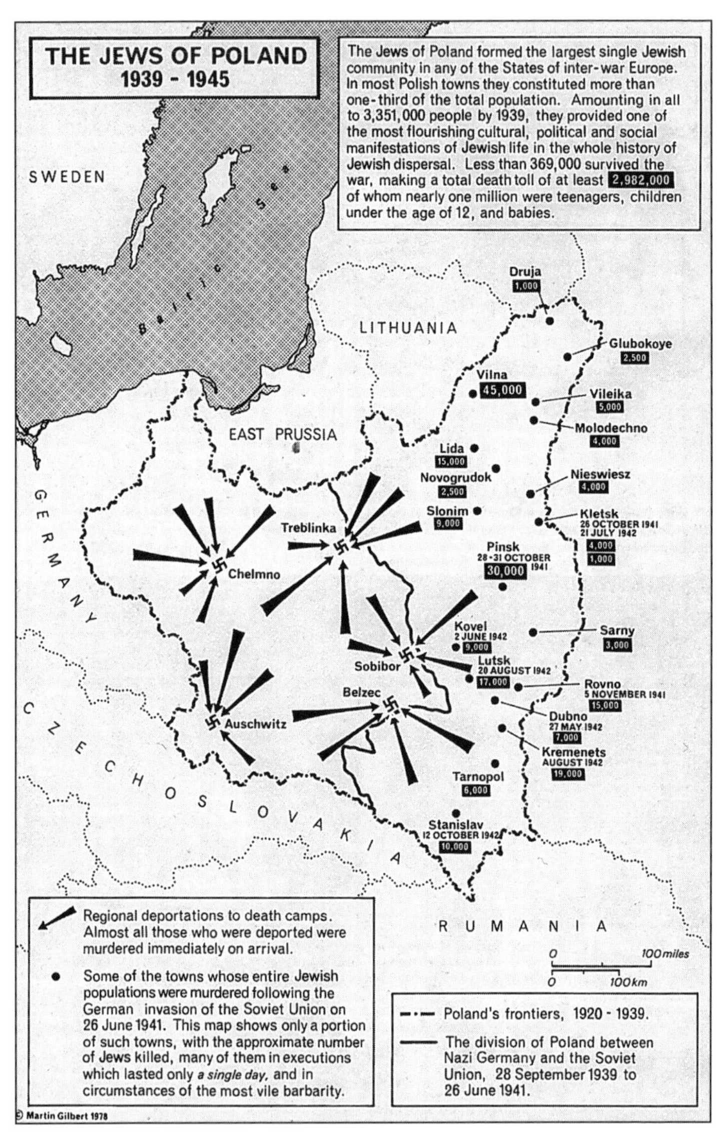
THE JEWS OF POLAND
1939 - 1945
The Jews of Poland formed the largest single Jewish community in any of the States of inter-war Europe. In most Polish towns they constituted more than one-third of the total population. Amounting in all to 3,351,000 people by 1939, they provided one of the most flourishing cultural, political and social manifestations of Jewish life in the whole history of Jewish dispersal. Less than 369,000 survived the war, making a total death toll of at least 2,982,000 of whom nearly one million were teenagers, children under the age of 12, and babies.
SWEDEN
Baltic Sea
LITHUANIA
EAST PRUSSIA
GERMANY
CZECHOSLOVAKIA
RUMANIA
Druja 1,000
Glubokoye 2,500
Vilna 45,000
Vileika 5,000
Molodechno 4,000
Lida 15,000
Novogrudok 2,500
Nieswiesz 4,000
Slonim 9,000
Kletsk 26 OCTOBER 1941 21 JULY 1942 4,000 1,000
Pinsk 28-31 OCTOBER 1941 30,000
Treblinka
Chelmno
Kovel 2 JUNE 1942 9,000
Sarny 3,000
Sobibor
Lutsk 20 AUGUST 1942 17,000
Rovno 5 NOVEMBER 1941 15,000
Belzec
Auschwitz
Dubno 27 MAY 1942 7,000
Kremenets AUGUST 1942 19,000
Tarnopol 6,000
Stanislav 12 OCTOBER 1942 10,000
Regional deportations to death camps. Almost all those who were deported were murdered immediately on arrival.
Some of the towns whose entire Jewish populations were murdered following the German invasion of the Soviet Union on 26 June 1941. This map shows only a portion of such towns, with the approximate number of Jews killed, many of them in executions which lasted only a single day, and in circumstances of the most vile barbarity.
0 100 miles
0 100 km
Poland's frontiers, 1920 - 1939.
The division of Poland between Nazi Germany and the Soviet Union, 28 September 1939 to 26 June 1941.
© Martin Gilbert 1978

Courtesy of Martin Gilbert.

JEWISH GHETTOS IN POLAND
JEWS FORCED INTO GHETTOS, OCTOBER 1939 TO DECEMBER 1940
Plonsk
August 1940
River Bug
Wloclawek
November 1940
River Vistula
Wolomin
15 November 1940
WARTHEGAU
Zychlin
13 July 1940
Warsaw
15 November 1940
Siedice
5 May 1940
Kutno
16 June 1940
Tuliszkow
January 1940
Kolo
December 1940
Bolimow
11 June 1940
Chocz
March 1940
Glowno
29 December 1940
Lodz
1 May 1940
Kozminek
January 1940
Lutomiersk
July 1940
Deblin
April 1940
Tomaszow
1 June 1940
Zdunska Wola
September 1940
Piotrkow
28 October 1939
THE GENERAL GOVERNMENT
Radomsko
20 December 1939
Czestochowa
March 1940
Chmielnik
March 1940
Jedrzejow
January 1940
Pinczow
February 1940
River Vistula
0 miles 40
0 kilometres 60
© Martin Gilbert 1982

Courtesy of Martin Gilbert.

THE CONCENTRATION CAMPS
Between 1939 and 1945, six million unarmed and innocent Jewish civilians - men, women, children and babies - were murdered in Nazi-controlled Europe, as part of a deliberate policy to destroy all traces of Jewish life and culture. As many as two million of these were killed in their own towns and villages, some confined in ghettoes where death by slow starvation was a deliberate Nazi policy, others taken to be shot at mass-murder sites near where they lived. The remaining four million Jews were forced from their homes and taken by train to distant concentration camps, where they were murdered by being worked to death, starved to death, beaten to death, shot, or gassed.
North Sea
Baltic Sea
Vaivara
Klooga
ESTONIA
LATVIA
LITHUANIA
USSR
Stutthof
Neuengamme
Ravensbrück
Bergen-Belsen
Sachsenhausen
Chelmno
Treblinka
POLAND
Sobibor
Mittelbau Dora
Gross Rosen
Maidanek
Buchenwald
Auschwitz
GERMANY
Belzec
Flossenberg
Plaszow
CZECHOSLOVAKIA
Natzweiler
Dachau
FRANCE
Mauthausen
AUSTRIA
HUNGARY
RUMANIA
Gospič
Jasenovac
YUGOSLAVIA
Sajmište
ITALY
Adriatic Sea
Among the hundreds of thousands of *non*-Jews sent by the Nazis to concentration camps were anti-Nazis, Jehovah's Witnesses, homosexuals, the mentally ill, and the chronically sick. In addition, more than 250,000 Gypsies were murdered, in a Nazi attempt to eliminate Gypsies as well as Jews from the map of Europe.
Auschwitz concentration camp in which more than 4 *million* people were murdered between 1941 and 1944, including Jews, Gypsies, and Soviet prisoners-of-war.
Camps set up solely for the murder of Jews.
Other camps in which Jews and non-Jews were put to forced labour, starved, tortured, and murdered in conditions of the worst imaginable cruelty. Most of these camps had "satellite" labour camps nearby.
In many of the camps shown here so-called "medical" experiments were carried out, without anaesthetics, solely to satisfy the curiosity and sadism of the doctors. Hundreds of otherwise healthy "patients" were tortured and murdered during these experiments.
0 100 miles
0 100 km
© Martin Gilbert 1978

Courtesy of Martin Gilbert.

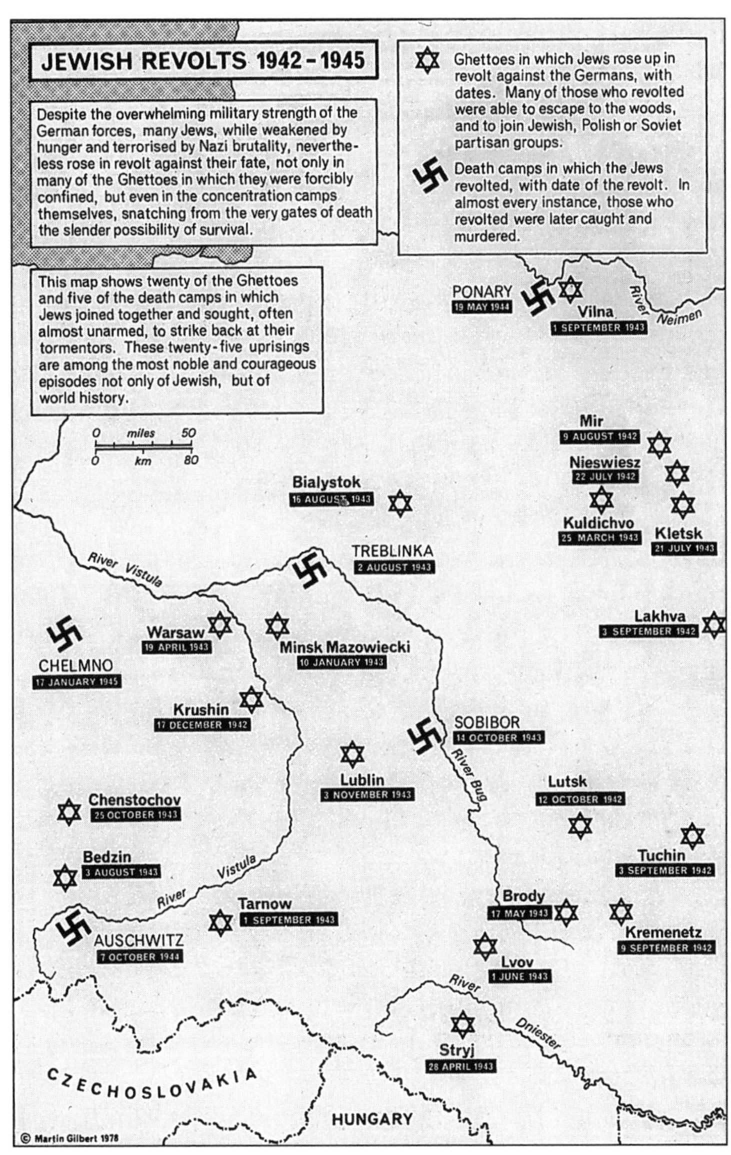
JEWISH REVOLTS 1942–1945
Despite the overwhelming military strength of the German forces, many Jews, while weakened by hunger and terrorised by Nazi brutality, nevertheless rose in revolt against their fate, not only in many of the Ghettoes in which they were forcibly confined, but even in the concentration camps themselves, snatching from the very gates of death the slender possibility of survival.
Ghettoes in which Jews rose up in revolt against the Germans, with dates. Many of those who revolted were able to escape to the woods, and to join Jewish, Polish or Soviet partisan groups.
Death camps in which the Jews revolted, with date of the revolt. In almost every instance, those who revolted were later caught and murdered.
This map shows twenty of the Ghettoes and five of the death camps in which Jews joined together and sought, often almost unarmed, to strike back at their tormentors. These twenty-five uprisings are among the most noble and courageous episodes not only of Jewish, but of world history.
0 miles 50
0 km 80
PONARY
19 MAY 1944
Vilna
1 SEPTEMBER 1943
River Neimen
Mir
9 AUGUST 1942
Nieswiesz
22 JULY 1942
Kuldichvo
25 MARCH 1943
Kletsk
21 JULY 1943
Bialystok
16 AUGUST 1943
TREBLINKA
2 AUGUST 1943
River Vistula
Lakhva
3 SEPTEMBER 1942
Warsaw
19 APRIL 1943
Minsk Mazowiecki
10 JANUARY 1943
CHELMNO
17 JANUARY 1945
Krushin
17 DECEMBER 1942
SOBIBOR
14 OCTOBER 1943
River Bug
Lublin
3 NOVEMBER 1943
Lutsk
12 OCTOBER 1942
Chenstochov
25 OCTOBER 1943
Tuchin
3 SEPTEMBER 1942
Bedzin
3 AUGUST 1943
River Vistula
Tarnow
1 SEPTEMBER 1943
Brody
17 MAY 1943
Kremenetz
9 SEPTEMBER 1942
AUSCHWITZ
7 OCTOBER 1944
Lvov
1 JUNE 1943
River Dniester
Stryj
28 APRIL 1943
CZECHOSLOVAKIA
HUNGARY
© Martin Gilbert 1978

Courtesy of Martin Gilbert.

POLISH JEWRY TODAY

Following the Six-Day War in 1967, relations between communist-ruled Poland and Israel were formally broken—an act that instantly separated the strongly knit Jewish communities of the two nations. Twenty years passed before the respective countries' governments were able to reach a new accord. With political ties finally restored, the link between the Jewries of Poland and Israel was quickly reestablished. A new era dawned with the nonstop flight of El Al Israel Airlines' Serial #4X-ABN from Warsaw to Tel Aviv on October 22, 1987. Shortly thereafter, Lot Polish Airlines inaugurated regular service between the two countries.

Since then, thousands of Israelis—many of them young—have visited Poland in order to search out their roots, to learn the tragic history of the Shoah, and to follow in the footsteps of American, Canadian, and European Jews by undertaking the pilgrimage to Kever Avot. The variety of these pilgrims' nationalities underscores the fact that, of the more than fifteen million Jews in the world today, half are traditionally linked with the heritage of the Polish Jewry.

There remains only a tiny Jewish community in modern Poland, probably well under 10,000 members. This total includes some modern-day "Marranos," of whom 5,000 maintain an active contact with Jewish institutions. All that is left of the vanished world is its heritage, monuments, and cemeteries.

Jewish life in Warsaw now centers around the Jewish Religious Organization (*Zwiazek Religijny Wyznania Mojzeszowego*), located next to the renovated Nozyk Synagogue on Twarda Street; and around the Cultural Association (*Towarzystwo Kulturalne Zydow w Polsce*), located at Plac Grzybowski next to the Yiddish Theater. The same building houses *Folks-Sztym*, a Jewish newspaper published in Yiddish and Polish, and *Midrash*, a monthly magazine edited by Konstanty Geber.

The Cultural Association also provides a home for the Esther Rachel Kaminska State Jewish Theater—the only state-subsidized Jewish theater in the world. Many Poles and foreigners attend its performances, for which earphones are provided for simultaneous translations in Polish. (Unfortunately, no other translations are currently offered.)

Small communities, or "active" synagogues, still exist in Bielsko-Biala, Bytom, Cracow, Czestochowa, Dzierzoniow, Gliwice, Katowice, Legnica, Lodz, Lublin, Szczecin, Walbrzych, Wroclaw, and Zary.

An organization deserving special mention is JDC—the American Jewish Joint Distribution Committee, or JOINT. Since its return to Poland in 1981, this group has played an important role in the country's Jewish life. Today, its programs reach approximately 4,500 Jews whose average age is 78. JDC provides cash relief for the impoverished, health services that are not available locally—medicine, hearing aids, and eyeglasses, among other things—and free meals. Its eight kosher kitchens currently serve 75,000 meals per year.

JDC programs also support weekly cultural activities in Jewish clubs: films followed by lectures, evenings of music, lectures with slides, and performances by the Yiddish Theater. In addition, the organization contributes to the Jewish Religious Congregation, which makes religious supplies such as matzot, lulavim, and ethrogim available to the community.

Since 1987, JDC has supported a program for young people between the ages of 20 and 45 as well. Generally the children of mixed marriages, they have begun to rediscover and explore their Jewish roots. They attend lectures in Jewish culture and tradition, as well as study Hebrew and Yiddish. By 1990, approximately 350 young people had participated in this program.

Also established in 1987, the Ronald S. Lauder Foundation has become vital to the support of Polish Jewry's remnants. The activities and programs of the foundation for Jewish children are integral and manifold: Jewish Community Youth Centers in Cracow, Gdansk, Lodz, Warsaw, and Wroclaw; educational retreat and summer camps in Srodborow and Rychwald; the provision of religious leadership and books for the Lauder Morasha School in Warsaw; and the organization of such events as concerts. The foundation has also established the Genealogy Project and The Museum of the History of Polish Jews (both in Warsaw), the International Auschwitz-Birkenau Preservation Project, and the World Monuments Fund. The latter project is dedicated to the restoration of historic buildings such as the magnificent Tempel Synagogue in Cracow.

According to a 1974 survey of the Polish Ministry of Religions, only 22 of the country's 434 Jewish cemeteries were in relatively good condition. Seventy-eight lay on the brink of complete destruction, while the rest were at least partially damaged.

Other "Jewish-oriented" organizations exist in Poland as well. The International Janusz Korczak Society honors Dr. Janusz Korczak (Henryk Goldszmit), who died in Treblinka with the children from his orphanage. Dr. Korczak was an internationally known educator and author of children's books. The Poles consider him a national hero as much as a Jewish one, and hundreds of educational and youth institutions bear his name. The society cooperates closely with Kibbutz Lochamey Hagetaot.

As of January 1, 1999, Yad Vashem recognized 5,260 Polish nationals as "Righteous among the Nations"—or 32% of the 16,526 honored. The Netherlands and France were second (25%) and third (11%) in honors.[1]

After a painful amnesia of some 40 years on matters Jewish, there is now an unusual interest in the subject, particularly among the Polish intelligentsia. Spurred by Poland's recovered sovereignty in 1989, a number of books have been published on Judaism, Shoah, and even Jewish cooking. Some are in English and German, but the bulk of them are in Polish. There is even a publishing firm that specializes in the translation of Hebrew literature into Polish.

Another sign of the renaissance in Jewish interest is the establishment of the Institute for Polish-Jewish Studies at the famous Jagiellonian University—one of the oldest universities in Europe. The institute runs under the directorship of the university's former rector, Prof. Jozef Gierowski, and with the assistance of the historian, Joachim Russek. Warsaw University, for its part, has established a Department of Jewish Culture headed by the known historian, Dr. Jerzy Tomaszewski.

The world-famous movie producer Andrzej Wajda has staged *Dybuk* in both Jerusalem and Cracow. He has also

1. A report issued by the Main Commission for the Investigation of Crimes against the Polish Nation documents the death of 704 Polish citizens for helping Jews during World War II. The list does not include the German "pacification" of Polish villages that helped the Jews.

The list of Poles who rescued Jews cannot be quite complete. Only a fraction of the 704 documented deaths are recognized by Yad Vashem. This discrepancy is partially explained by Yad Vashem's criteria, which require testimony from Jews who received assistance from Gentiles. When the Germans killed the Polish rescuers along with their Jewish charges, there obviously was no one alive to make the required statement(s).

completed a biopic on Janusz Korczak, and staged a musical based on Bashevis Singer's book, *Magician of Lublin*, in 1994.

Israeli theatrical groups and the Israeli Philharmonic frequently visit Poland. During one visit, world-renowned violinist Itzhak Perlman and the Philharmonic gave an impromptu recital at the Femina Cinema—the same building at which the Jewish Symphony Orchestra performed for residents of the Warsaw Ghetto (1940–1942).

In the United States, a foundation for Polish-Jewish studies has been inaugurated under the leadership of author, Jerzy Kosinski; and Oxford publishes *Polin*, a Polish-Jewish journal that results from the collaboration of scholars in England, Israel, Poland, and the United States.

The Polish-Israel Friendship League was recently created by a number of young leading members of the Jewish community. Once headed by the late Senator Andrzej Szczypiorski (author of *The Beautiful Mrs. Seidenman*), the league boasts the membership of Prof. Jozef Gierowski, Dr. Andrzej Friedman, and Prof. Jerzy Tomaszewski.

As the complex and painful Polish-Jewish relations have inched toward a better understanding, they have suffered a series of setbacks. One such example is the controversy over the Carmelite Convent of Auschwitz. The new democracy has also given freedom of expression to the Rightist movement of the "Grünwald" type.

Yet, there are some powerful indications that a new chapter has begun in Polish-Jewish relations, including but not limited to President Lech Walesa's historic visit to Israel in 1992. A memorial to the Jews of Staszov was erected on the fiftieth anniversary of their deportation; and another painfully tragic fiftieth anniversary—that of the Warsaw Ghetto Uprising in 1943—was marked with the minting of a commemorative silver coin.

Modern Polish Jewry.

CHAPTER 3

Contributors and Contributions

The contributions of Polish Jewry have covered many fields of human endeavor. Volumes would be necessary to deal with such an array of rich subjects, necessitating that only a few renowned contributors in each area may be mentioned.

LEADERS & MOVEMENTS

Haskalah Movement

Dubno, Solomon Ben Yoel (1738–1813)
Lewin, Menahem Mendel of Satanow (1750–1823)
Maimon, Solomon (1754–1800)
Marense, Israel Ben Moses Halevy (c. 1700–1772)

Hassidic Movement

Ben-Eliezer, Israel (Ba'al Shem Tov) (1700–1760)
Joseph, Rabbi Jacob of Polomoye (1842–1902)

Zionist Movement

Begin, Menachem (1913–1992)
- prime minister of Israel (1977–1983)

Ben-Gurion, David (1886–1973)
- first prime minister of Israel (1949–1953; 1955–1963)

Gruenbaum, Itzhak (1879–1970)

Rosmaryn, Henryk (1882–1955)

Shamir, Itzhak (1915–)
- ➢ prime minister of Israel (1983–1984; 1986–1992)

Sommerstein, Emil (1883–1957)

Thon, Rabbi Osias (1870–1936)

LITERATURE

Men of Letters

Mortkowicz, Jakub (1876–1931)
- ➢ co-founder of the Polish Book House and Ruch Railway Bookshops, which can still be seen throughout present–day Poland

Natanson, Bronislaw (1865–1906)
- ➢ generous patron of Polish literature who encouraged and published the works of renowned writers: Stefan Zeromski, Eliza Orzeszkowa, and Nobel Prize winner, Wladyslaw Reymont

Orgelbrand, Samuel (1810–1868)
- ➢ publisher of the *Universal Encyclopaedia* (1858)

Sztybel, Abraham Joseph (1884–1946)
- ➢ generous patron of Hebrew literature

Telz, Napoleon (Naphtali) (1866–1943)
- ➢ publisher of a variety of newspapers, including *Dziennik Krakowski*, *Dziennik Poranny*, and *Naprzod*

Poets

Grynberg, Henryk (1936–)
Lesmian, Boleslaw (1878–1937)
Manger, Itzik (1901–1969)
Slonimski, Anatol (1895–1976)
Stern, Anatol (1899–1968)
Tuwim, Julian (1894–1953)
Wazyk, Adam (1905–1982)
Wittlin, Joseph (1896–1976)

Polish-Language Writers

Gorska, Halina (1898–1942)
Korczak, Janusz (1878–1942)
Kosinski, Jerzy (1933–1991)
Lutowski, Jerzy (1923–)
Schulz, Bruno (1892–1942)
Winawer, Bruno (1883–1944)
Wygodzki, Stanislaw (1907–)

Hebrew Translators of Polish Works

Abraham, Chaim Ben (Wladyslaw Reymont)
Frank, E.N. & A. Lewinson, (Henryk Sienkewicz)
Klaczko, Judah Julian & Lichtenbaym, J. (Adam Mickiewicz)

Yiddish and Hebrew Writers

Abramovitschm, Shalom Jacob (Mendele Mocher Sefarim) (1836–1917)
Asch, Sholem (1880–1957)
Berdyczewski, Micha Josef (1865–1921)
Bershadsky, Isaiah (1871–1908)
Bialik, Chaim Nachman (1873–1934)
Greenberg, Uri Zvi (1896–1981)
Katzenelson, Itzhak (1886–1944)
Opatoshu, Jopseph (1886–1954)
Perec, Icchak Leib (1851–1915)
Shalom Aleichem (1859–1916)
Singer, Isaac Bashevis (1904–1991)
Zeitlin, Hillel (1871–1942)

MUSIC AND THEATER

Cantors

Bernsztajin, Moshe Abraham
Gerszowich, Eliezier
Kusewicki, Moshe
Morogowski, Jakub Shmuel
Rosenblat, Josele (American who frequently visited Poland)
Szerman, Pinchas

Choirs

In the period between the World Wars, there were a number of choirs throughout Poland. The most famous of these was the Lodz Choir's "Hazamir" Nightingale. In addition, David Ajzensztadt led a 100-person choir at the

Tlomackie Synagogue of Warsaw, from which its concerts were broadcast over the radio. Famous choirmasters of the period include:

Bajgelman, Dawid (1887–1944)
Dswidowica, Abraham Cwi (1877–1942)
Fajwyszys, Israel (1887–1942)
Gladszrein, Jakub (1885–1942)
Liow, Leo (1878–1963)
Sliep, Abraham (1884–1942)
Szneur, Mosze (1885–1942)

Most of these individuals perished in the Holocaust.

Composers

Bialstocki, Zygmunt

- ➢ composer of hits sung by Bing Crosby and Doris Day

Petersburski, Jerzy

- ➢ writer of renowned "Donna Clara" and "Amour Disait Folie," which were part of Edith Piaf's repertoire.

Folk Artists and Singers

Fajerman, Mordko (Mordechai) (1810–1870)

- ➢ prototype of Jankiel in *Pan Tadeusz*, the Polish national epic by Adam Mickiewicz

Gebirtig, Mordechai (1877–1942)

- ➢ composer of "S'brent Unzer Shtetl Brent" ("Our Town is on Fire"), which became the hymn of the fighting ghettos (see page 136).

Musicians

Furmanski, Adam
Kochanski, Eli (1885–1942)
Kochanski, Pawel (1887–1934)
Piatigorski, Grzegosz (1903–1976)

Theater Masters

Kaminska, Esther Rachel (1868–1925)
- ➢ "Mother of the Yiddish Theater"

Kaminska, Ida (1899–1980)
- ➢ Esther's daughter, reestablished her mother's theater after WWII

Turkow, Zygmunt (1896–1970)
- ➢ Ida's husband, managed the revived theater

PAINTING

Painters

The collection of the Museum of Jewish Art, attached to the Jewish Historical Institute, includes paintings by such renowned artists as Adolf Behrman, Jan Gotard, Maurycy Gottlieb, Marcin Kitz, Artur Markowicz, Bruno Schulz, Jonasz Stern, Maurycy Trebacz, and Marek Wlodarski. It also boasts sculptures and metalworks by Jozef Gabowicz, Henryk Glicenszsten, Romauld Gruszczynski, Henryk Kuna, Abraham Ostrzega, Jozek Sliwiak, and Alina Szapocznikow.

Some paintings dealing with Jewish themes can be viewed at a variety of other museums, including the following institutions:

Museums

National Museum in Warsaw (3 Aleje Jerozolimskie)

- ➢ *The Anger of Saul with David* by Antoni Brodowski (1784–1832)
- ➢ *Casimir the Great and Jews* by Wojciech Gerson (1831–1901)
- ➢ *Jewish Feast* (*Swieto Trabek; Tashlich*) by Aleksander Gierymski (1850–1901) [front cover]
- ➢ *Umbrella and the Invisible* by Tadeusz Kantor (1915–1990)
- ➢ *Portrait of Young Girl* by Mojzesz (Moise) Kisling (1891–1953)
- ➢ *Death of Berek Joselewicz* by Henryk Pillati (1832–1894)

National Museum (Muzeum Narodowe) in Cracow, Ulica 3 Maja: 1

- ➢ *Ahasverus* by Maurycy Gottlieb (1856–1879)
- ➢ *The Maccabees* by Wojciech Korneli Stattler (1800–1875)

National Museum in Poznan

- ➢ *Ramamagauga* by Tadeusz Kantor

Museum of Art in Lodz

- ➢ *A Worthless Cargo* by Jerzy Krawczyk

Lublin Palace

- ➢ *Bringing Jews to Poland* by Jan Matejko (1838–1893)

In the summer of 1989, the National Gallery in Cracow organized a massive exhibition entitled "The Jews of Poland." It included 1,400 paintings that dealt with Jewish themes or were painted by Jewish artists—all of which came from museums and other educational institutions throughout Poland. Among them were the following:

The Art Museum in Lodz
The Czartoryski Collection in Cracow
The Jagiellonian University in Cracow
The Jewish Historical Institute in Warsaw
The National Gallery in Cracow
The National Gallery in Poznan
The National Gallery in Warsaw
The National Gallery in Wroclaw
The National Library in Warsaw

The exhibition included these giants of Polish art:

Gierymski, Aleksander
Gottlieb, Maurycy
Lesser, Aleksander (1814–1884)
Malczewski, Jacek (1854–1929)
Matejko, Jan (national painter of Poland)

The paintings of Aleksander Sochaczewski (1843–1923) that depict the Polish martyrdom in Siberia are on permanent exhibit at the Warsaw Citadel. A scaled-down version of the exhibition subsequently moved to the Zacheta Gallery in Warsaw.

STUDIES

Historians

Balaban, Prof. Meir (1877–1942)—Jewish History
Heschel, Dr. Abraham (1907–1972)—Philosopher of Religion

Schorr, Prof. Moses (1874–1942)—Bible and Semetic Languages
Stein, Prof. Edmund (1895–1943)—Hellenistic and Midrash Studies
Weiss, Dr. Abraham (1895–1970)—Archaeology

Judaic Studies

Anshel of Cracow (first half of 16th c.)
- ➢ publisher of the first Yiddish book (1534), used to spread knowledge of the Bible among women who knew no Hebrew

Falk, Yehousha Ben Alexander Hachocen (1550–1614)
- ➢ rector of Lvov (Lwow) Yeshiva and commentator upon the *Shulkhan Arukh*

Frank, Jakob (1726–1791)
- ➢ leader of the Frankist Movement and false Messiah

Heller, Yom Tov Lippman (1579–1654)
- ➢ commentator of the *Misnah*

Horowitz of Kazimierz (1632–1689)
- ➢ author of *Schnei Luhot Habrith*

Isserless, Moses (Remu) (1530–1572)
- ➢ follower of Maimonides, head of Cracow Yeshiva, and author of an adaptation of *Schulchan Arukh* to meet the needs of the Ashkenazi Jews

Jacob of Belzyce (16th c.)
- ➢ author of *Dialogue with Marcin Czechowic*

Jaffe, Mordechai (1530–1612)
- ➢ author of *Levushim*

Muelhausen, Yom Tov Lippman of Cracow (15th c.)
- ➢ author of *Sefer Hanitzachon*

Pollack, Rabbi Jacob of Cracow (d. 1530)
- ➢ establisher of the principle of *pilpul* (pepper), a method in theological writing

Rebecca
- ➢ daughter of Rabbi Meir Tikitner (of Tykocin) and publisher of instruction and song books for women

Troki, Isaac Abraham the Karaite (1533–1594)
- ➢ author of *Hizuk Emunah*

Zalman, Rabbi Elijah Ben Solomon (1720–1797)
- ➢ Gaon of Villa, the "Enlightened Talmudist"

Other renowned rabbis include:
- ➢ Abraham Ben Shabbetai Horowitz (16th c.)
- ➢ Mordechai Ben Abraham Jaffe (1532–1612)
- ➢ Jacob Ben Samuel Bunim Koppelman (1555–1598)
- ➢ Solomon Luria (1510–1573)

TRADES AND PROFESSIONS

Doctors of Polish Kings

Albert, John—*Casimir the Jagiellon*
Ashkenazi, Solomon—*Sigismund Augustus*
De Yonah, Menahem Simha Emmanuel—*John III Sobieski*

Minters

Jews were minters to several Polish kings and dukes. Some early twelfth-century coins bear the names of Abraham, Josef, Yaacov, and Menahem, as well as the words *Beracha*, *Beracha Vehatzlaha*, and *Beracha Tova*, among others. One coin is inscribed *Beracha Casi*, or "Blessing to Casimir." These "Hebrew" coins were minted in Poland a full thousand years after the last ones had been produced by Bar Kochba.

The Jewish Press

Between 1918 and 1939, 30 dailies and 130 Jewish periodicals were published in three languages. Among them were *Nasz Kurier*, *Nasz Przeglad*, *Maly Przeglad* (edited by Janusz Korczak), *Dzienik Warszawski*, *Nasz Glos Warszawy*, and the *Yiddish Telegrafen Agentur* (JTA). The latter paper was founded by Mendel Moses and still exists today in the United States.

In addition to the "official" *Gazeta Zydowska*, some 70 clandestine newspapers were published between 1940 and 1943. At the present time, the Cultural Social Union publishes *Yiddish Weekly Folks Sztym*, the only Yiddish weekly in the former Eastern Bloc.

To sum up what remains of such a rich heritage, one can quote a poem of Anton Slonimski:

> Gone now are those little towns where the
>   shoemaker was a poet,
> The watchmaker a philosopher, the barber a
>   troubadour.
> Gone now are those little towns where the wind joined
> Biblical songs with Polish tunes and Slavic rue,

Where old Jews in orchards in the shade of cherry trees
Lamented for the holy walls of Jerusalem.
Gone now are those little towns, though the poetic mists,
The moons, winds, ponds, and stars above them
Have recorded in the blood of centuries the tragic tales,
The histories of the two saddest nations on earth.

CHAPTER 4

Glossary of Polish Jewry

A

Aleksandrow Lodzki (Aleksander)—west of Lodz

Ulica Gorna is the location of a Jewish cemetery that was established in 1822. Only a few graves have survived, that of Tzadik Dancygier among them.

Augustow—north of Bialystok

There were 4,000 Jews in residence here on the eve of WWII, most of whom traded in timber. The ghetto was established in October 1941, and liquidated ten months later by deportations to Treblinka and Auschwitz. A devastated cemetery features a memorial stone for Shoah victims.

Auschwitz (Oswiecim)

For a description of the town of Oswiecim see page 88.

Auschwitz-Birkenau (Oswiecim-Brzezinka)

The concentration, death, and work camp at Oswiecim—known by the German title *Konzentrationslager Auschwitz*—was established on April 27, 1940 on Himmler's orders. The biggest Nazi death factory (*Vernichtungslager*), it was a complex of 40 camps, where up to 60,000 people were murdered each day.

The Entrance Gate to Auschwitz-Birkenau.

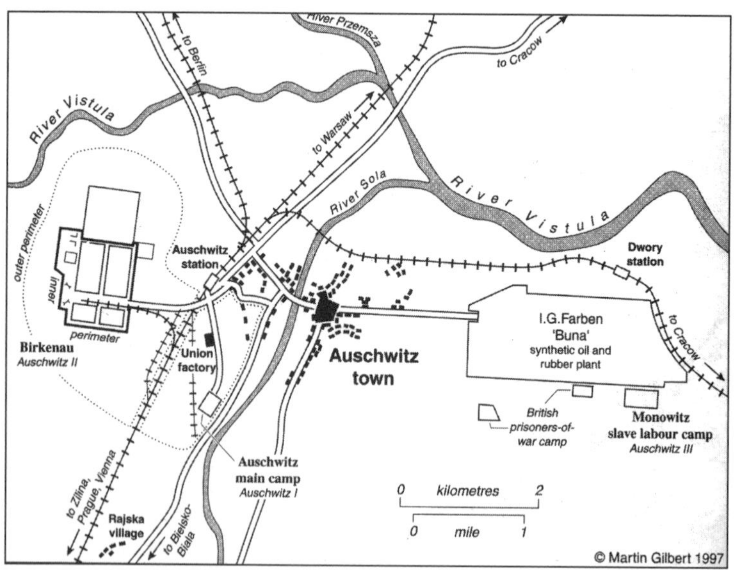

The Auschwitz Concentration Camp Area. Courtesy of Martin Gilbert.

In this area of 25 square miles, slightly more than a one-hour drive from Cracow, the Nazis killed four million people—a total that includes three million Jews.

The trains arrived at Birkenau (Brzezinka), a few miles from Oswiecim. At the spot where the railway ramp ended and "selection" occurred, there stands a restored monument that honors the four million who perished here. The commemoration stones are inscribed in 18 languages—Hebrew, Polish, and Yiddish among them.

Remnants of the crematoria blown up by the Nazis can be seen in the area of the monument. On both sides of the tracks stand the remains of the wooden barracks that housed the prisoners.

On the Auschwitz side, a Jewish martyrdom pavilion (Cell Block #27) memorializes Hitler's six million Jewish victims. At the door stands a guest book that has been signed by thousands of visitors to the pavilion. At the exit is an inscribed slab: "And the Lord said unto Cain, 'Where is Abel thy brother?' And He said, 'What has thou done? The voice of thy brother crieth unto Me from the ground.'" This pavilion is one of a number of "national" pavilions; others serve as a museum of the death factory.

A CHRONOLOGY OF THE AUSCHWITZ COMPLEX

1940

4-27 Heinrich Himmler, SS Commander-in-Chief, orders the construction of a concentration camp on the site of the former Polish artillery barracks. The factors leading to this decision are the potential to expand the camp, the site's relative isolation, and its railway connections to many parts of Europe.

5-4 Rudolf Hoess is officially appointed commander of Auschwitz.

5-20 First inmates are registered at Auschwitz: 30 convicted German criminals who would serve as Kapos, or inmate supervisors who enforced camp policy.

6-14 First transport of 728 Polish political prisoners arrives from Tarnow Prison.

1941

3-1 More than 10,000 inmates are interned at Auschwitz. Heinrich Himmler visits the camp, accompanied by officials of the I.G. Farben Company, a major German industrial firm. Himmler orders that the camp be expanded to hold 30,000 inmates, and that auxilliary camps be established, including the Buna Camp that would eventually house 10,000 prisoners for I.G. Farben.

Summer Himmler orders Hoess to make Auschwitz the center of the "Final Solution of the Jewish Question"—the Nazi euphemism for the systematic extermination of Jews.

9-3 First experiments with the poisonous gas, Zyklon B, are conducted in order to find a method for quickly killing large numbers of people. The first victims are sick inmates and Russian POWs.

10-14 Construction of a branch camp begins at Birkenau. It is originally intended for Russian POWs, 10,000 of whom are already imprisoned at Auschwitz.

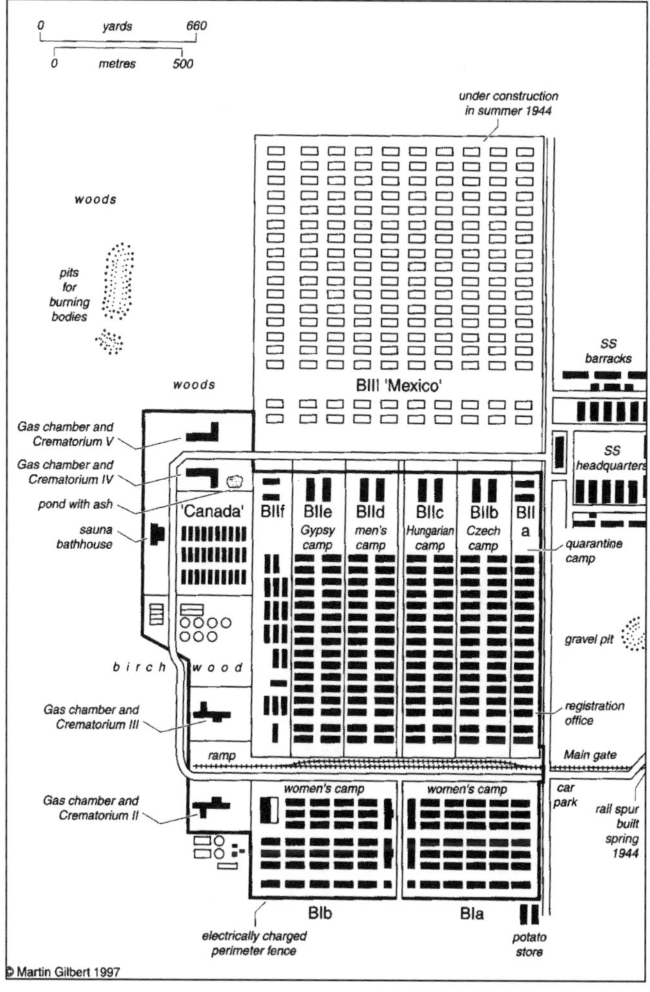

Birkenau. Courtesy of Martin Gilbert.

1942

1-1 By this date, in accordance with Nazi plans, the majority of all new arrivals to the camp are Jewish. Beginning of the mass murder of Jews at Birkenau with the use of Zyklon B.

3-26 First transport of Jews from Western Europe (France) arrives at Auschwitz.

3-30 First women inmates arrive at women's camp, including 999 German women from Ravensbruck and 999 Jewish women from Slovakia.

July Himmler's second visit includes an inspection of Birkenau, where he witnesses the gassing of inmates in two cottages that had been converted to improvised gas chambers. Orders are issued to the Topf und Soehne Company to construct four large crematoria with adjoining gas chambers.

7-17 First transport of Dutch Jews arrives.

8-5 First transport of Belgian Jews arrives.

1943

2-26 Gypsy camp established at Birkenau—one of the 40 satellite camps created during 1942 and 1943. Twenty-eight of these camps supply slave labor to adjacent industrial plants.

3-15 Deportation of Greek Jews from Salonika to Auschwitz begins.

March – June Previously ordered and tested crematoria are put into operation. The capacity of the larger two gas chambers is 2,000 persons each.

October After the partial German occupation of Italy, approximately 8,500 Jews are captured and sent to Auschwitz.

*** By the end of 1943, Jews represent the majority of inmates at Auschwitz-Birkenau.

1944

July – August 425,000 Hungarian Jews are sent to Auschwitz, 85% of whom are killed upon arrival.

August As a result of the Red Army's advances on the Eastern Front, orders are given to phase out the activities at Auschwitz and to eliminate all traces of its operations.

10-7 Crematorium Number Three is blown up, forcing a revolt of the Sonderkommando—the Jewish inmates who were forced to remove the bodies from the gas chambers. The revolt had initially planned to destroy all the crematoria, but timing factors prevented the actualization of this plan.

11-25 Nazis destroy the remaining crematoria and gas chambers.

1945

1-18 Evacuation of Auschwitz begins, prompting the infamous Death Marches (for those able to walk). Thousands die in these cruel and often aimless marches west towards Germany. Sick and disabled inmates are left behind.

1-27 Russian troops, under Jewish Colonel Grigori Elishawetzki, liberate Auschwitz and the approximately 7,650 prisoners who remained there.

B

Bakalarzewo

A Jewish cemetery here survives with a few gravestones.

Baranow Sandomierski (Bornow)—east of Kielce

The Jewish cemetery includes a mass grave of 60 Jews who were shot to death by the Germans.

Bedzin (Bendin)—near Katowice

The first Jews settled in Bedzin in the seventeenth century, and were immediately active in both industry and commerce. By the 1920s, they comprised a full 60% of the population.

The Germans destroyed the town's synagogue in the first days of September 1939. In May 1942, the first massive deportation to Auschwitz occurred. The ghetto was established in January 1943, and was liquidated just eight months later. During this last deportation, an armed resistance took place under the leadership of Frumka Plotnica, who was killed in action.

A tablet at the courthouse (22 Lipcanz 23) commemorates the 200 victims who were burned in the synagogue on September 9, 1939, after a Wehrmacht bombing.

Belzec

Belzec was a death camp established by the Germans in November 1941 (and first reported to the West by Jan Karski). Six hundred thousand persons—mainly Jews from Czechoslovakia, Germany, Hungary, Poland, and Romania—perished here. Upon liquidation of the camp in 1943, the Germans planted a forest in an attempt to cover up their crimes. A memorial was built in 1963. The sculptor was Roman Dylewski; the designer was Mieczyslaw Welter.

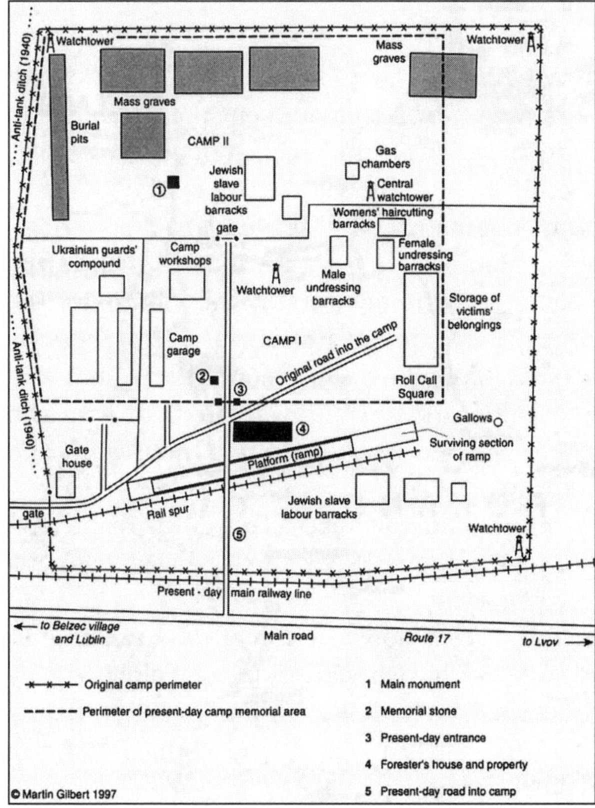

Belzec Camp. Courtesy of Martin Gilbert.

Berzniki

The town is home to a destroyed Jewish cemetery.

Biala Podlaska—east of Warsaw

A memorial located at the Jewish cemetery (on Ulica Nowa) commemorates 12,000 Jews from Biala Podlaska, Augustow, and Suwalki.

Bialowieza

Though both of the town's Jewish cemeteries have been destroyed, an obelisk has been erected in memory of Jews executed in August 1941.

Bialystok

The Jewish Cemetery on Zabia is part of a public park that is dominated by two large monuments: one commemorates the ghetto's dead, while the second honors Jewish partisans. The cemetery at Polnocna was established in 1890 and contains approximately 6,000 graves.

The Pogrom Memorial, a towering marble shaft in the old Jewish cemetery, commemorates the victims of the 1905 pogrom. The monument's inscription is a poem by the Hebrew poet, Zalman Shneour. Another memorial contains the ashes of 3,500 Jews killed during the Uprising, which was led by Mordechai Tenenbaum and Daniel Moszkowicz.

The Zamenhof Monument honors Dr. Ludwik Zamenhof, creator of the international Esperanto language, who was born in the city in 1859.

A plaque at the Press House, a former synagogue, commemorates the 3,000 Jewish victims burned alive on May 24, 1941. Inscribed in both Polish and Yiddish, it was affixed on the fifteenth anniversary of the Bialystok Ghetto Uprising (August 16, 1943).

Another memorial tablet honors the Jewish resistance fighter Itzhak Malmed at the exact spot (Malmeda 10) where the Germans killed him.

Rebuilt after the war, the synagogue at Piekna 3 now serves as a youth house. The Jewish school at Marchlewskiego 1, built about 1905, now functions as part of Warsaw University.

Biecz (Beitch)

A monument honoring Holocaust victims at the Jewish cemetery (at Tysiaclecia) was erected on the site of a mass grave. The synagogue is now a hotel.

Biedrzyce-Koziegłowy (Sypniewo Parish)

A tablet in the school courtyard marks the location of the work camp that existed from 1941 to 1942.

Bielsk Podlaski—south of Bialystok

The Jewish community here dates back to the fifteenth century. The first synagogue was built in 1542. In September 1939, Bielsk was home to a population of 6,000 Jews—a number that included many refugees from the West who escaped to what later became Soviet-occupied Poland.

The ghetto was established at the end of 1941, and liquidated in 1942 by deportation to Treblinka. The cemetery at Ulica Branska still contains about 100 matzevot.

Bielsko Biala (Bielitz-Biala)—west of Cracow

The ghetto established here in 1941 was liquidated in June 1940.

The cemetery (at Cieszynska 92) was established in 1849 with 400 graves. The congregation and house of worship currently stands at Mickiewicza 26.

Bielzyce (Belshitza)

A monument remembers the 1,000 Jews shot by the Germans upon the liquidation of the ghetto on May 8, 1943.

Nimrod Ariav, a native of Israel, erected a cemetery and a monument in October 1990 in order to honor his father, Arie Cygielman. Exactly 48 years earlier, the Germans had shot Mr. Cygielman in the square before the synagogue.

Biernatki (Zelazkow County)—north of Kalisz

An obelisk commemorates 125 Jews who were shot on October 10, 1941 in the nearby forest. Their remains now rest in the town's Jewish cemetery.

Bilgoraj—south of Lublin

Though the cemetery at Morowa has been completely destroyed, the cemetery at Konopnickiej has been restored through the efforts of the Lumerman family. The town's memorial honors Jewish, Polish, and Russian partisans who were executed in the woods of Rapy.

Bilgoraj is also the proud birthplace of Isaac Bashevis Singer.

Monument at Bielzyce, funded by N. Ariav.

Biskupiec

Remnants of a destroyed synagogue are to be found at Dzierzynskiego.

Bobowo—near Nowy Sacz

The nineteenth-century synagogue has been converted into a school. The town's Jewry has recently returned to the Hassidim of Bobowo.

Bochnia—east of Cracow

Jews first arrived in Bochnia in the fifteenth century, gradually growing until their pre-WWII population reached 3,500—none of whom would survive the war. Approximately 2,000 perished in Belzec, while the remaining members were killed at Auschwitz.

The cemetery, which was established in 1872 at Orackiej, contains 100 matzevot. On its grounds stands a monument honoring Holocaust victims, as well as a memorial for victims of mass executions.

The synagogue at Swierczewskiego now serves as an office building, while the synagogue at Warynskiego houses a restaurant called Sutoris.

Bodzentyn—west of Ostrowiec-Swietokrzyski

Jews immigrated to Bodzentyn in the nineteenth century. The ghetto was liquidated in November 1942, and its inhabitants deported to Treblinka. The famous diary of Dawidek Rubinowicz—the Polish equivalent of Anne Frank's diary—was found in this town.

The cemetery at Gora Miejska, established in 1867, still holds some 55 matzevot.

Borownica—south of Krasnik

At the Jewish cemetery, a stone marks the spot where 100 Jews from the work camp at Radymno were executed in October 1942.

Brzesko (Brigel)—east of Bochnia

Established in 1846, the cemetery features 100 matzevot. Its excellent condition and renovation are owed to the initiative of Abe Hirsch. An obelisk on the grounds marks the mass grave of some 500 Jews executed by the Germans.

The synagogue at Ulica Pusnika now houses a municipal library.

Bydgoszcz—west of Warsaw

Jews first arrived in this town in the eleventh and twelfth centuries. A synagogue was constructed in 1835; and by 1939, the Jewish community numbered some 25,000 persons. The main gate to Zachem Chemical Works commemorates British, Dutch, and Belgian POWs, as well as the Jews who died in Stutthof.

At Przyjemna 1 Wzgorze Wolnosci, *Cmentarz Bohaterow* (Heroes' Cemetery) bears a plaque that commemorates 2,500 Jewish inhabitants of the town.

The synagogue in Fordon is now a cinema.

Bytom—near Katowice

The Jewish presence here dates back to 1349; and approximately 1,400 Jews lived in the town on the eve of the German invasion.

The congregation is currently located at Smolenska 4; the house of worship stands at Plac Grunwaldzki 62. The Jewish cemetery lies at Piekarska 56, and contains about 1,000 graves in all.

C

Cecylowka—west of Deblin

A monument honors 54 victims who were locked up in a barn and burned by the Wehrmacht on September 13, 1939.

Checiny

The synagogue is now a cinema. The cemetery at Gora Zamkowa contains 150 graves, the oldest of which dates back to 1638.

Chelm—east of Lublin

The Jewish presence in Chelm can be traced back to 1442. Famous citizens of the town include Rabbi Yehuda Aron and Eliahu Baal Shem—names that underscore its previous importance as a center of Polish Jewry.

On the eve of WWII, 15,000 Jews resided in Chelm and they were served by two Jewish weeklies. The mass deportation occurred in 1942.

The synagogue now houses a technical school. The cemetery is located at Starosinska.

Chelmno (Cumhof on the Ner River)—northwest of Lodz

The camp at Chelmno was established on December 8, 1941, and operated until January 1945 as Sonderkommando Cumhof.

A monument to victims on the site of the camp marks the first death camp erected in occupied Poland by the Nazis, and memorializes 360,000 Jews—all but 20,000 of whom were from Poland. Among the other victims were Russian POWs and 88 Czech children from Lidice.

Chelmno Monument, designed by J. Stasinski and J. Buszkiewicz.

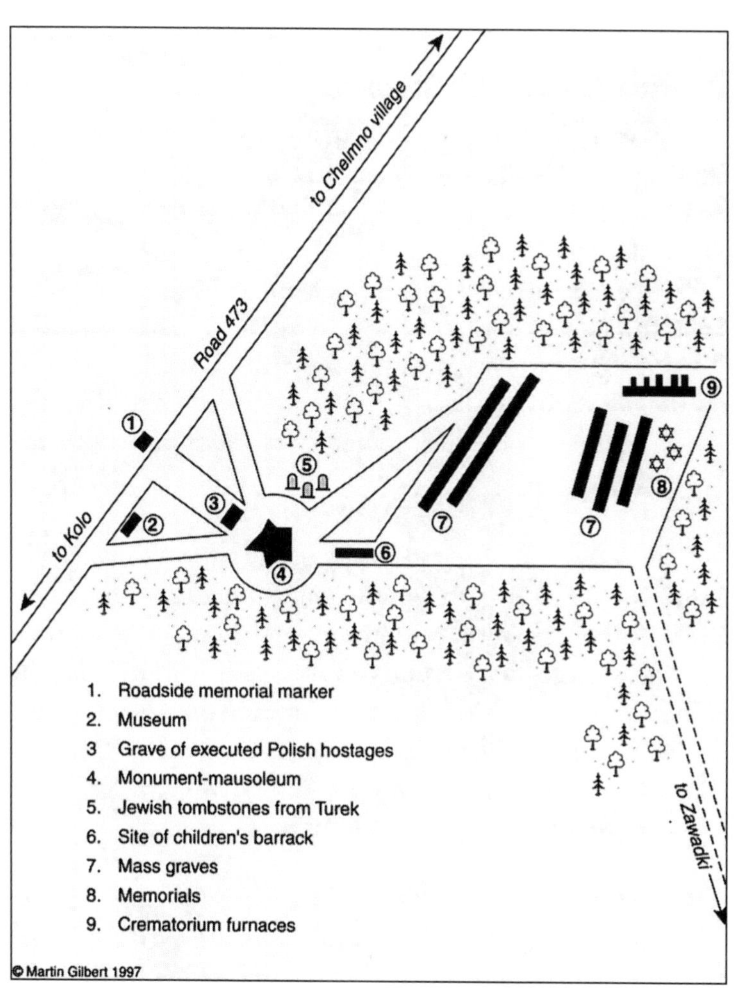

Chelmno. Courtesy of Martin Gilbert.

Another monument in front of the main Catholic Church honors the Jews who staged an unsuccessful revolt against the Nazis.

Chmielnik—south of Kielce

According to the 1921 census, 5,900 Jews lived in Chmielnik. The ghetto was established in April 1941, and liquidation occurred in 1943 by mass deportation to Treblinka.

A synagogue of great architectural value was built from 1630 to 1634.

Choroszcz

Its eighteenth-century cemetery contains 250 matzevot.

Chrzanow—west of Cracow

There were about 8,000 Jews in the town before WWII. Established in 1940, the ghetto was liquidated three years later. Most of the Jewish community perished in Auschwitz.

The synagogue currently serves as a warehouse. The cemetery at Podwale contains some 50 matzevot, while the cemetery at Borowcowa consists of approximately 1,000 graves.

The Chrzanow Museum features Judaica.

Ciechanow—north of Warsaw

The town's Jewish community dates back to the sixteenth century. The ghetto was liquidated by deportation to the Mlawa Ghetto, and from there to Auschwitz.

A plaque affixed to the parish house at Ulica Fabryczna commemorates the inmates of a penal camp. A devastated cemetery lies at Pulanska.

Ciechanowice

In a destroyed cemetery at Sienkiewicza stands a monument for Shoah victims. Reconstructed in 1954, a nineteenth-century synagogue at Mostowa now houses a furniture store.

Cieszanow—south of Zamosc

The synagogue at Skorupi 7 was established in 1889, and now serves as a warehouse. The town's Jewish cemetery has been completely destroyed.

Cieszyn—west of Cracow

A nearly destroyed synagogue stands at Ulica Hazlaska 2. Eighteenth- and nineteenth-century cemeteries on the same street contain 500 matzevot between them. A monument stands at the latter cemetery and marks the spot of a mass execution in 1944.

The tablet on the wall of the local school memorializes Jewish women who were imprisoned at a nearby camp in 1944.

Cracow (Krakow/Kroke)

See Chapter Five, page 131.

Czechowice-Dedzice—north of Bieszko Biala

At this former branch of the Auschwitz camp, a monument honors Jews who were shot by the Germans on the eve of liberation on January 19, 1945. The cemetery at Szkolna possesses 50 matzevot.

Czestochowa (Chenstchow)—northwest of Cracow

The Jewish community in Czestochowa goes back to the seventeenth century. The first Jewish settlers found employment in the textile and tapestry industries.

By 1765, 51 Jewish families called this town home. The year 1799 saw the establishment of a synagogue and a Jewish cemetery, which replaced a burial site in Janowo.

A more elaborate synagogue was built in 1899 at Spadek and Aleksandryjska Streets—a spot now occupied by the Czestochowa Philharmonic.

On the eve of WWII, the Jewish population of the town was 40,000. The town had a Jewish theater, which was funded by the Wohlberg family, and was situated as Aleje Najswietszei Mazii Panny 12.

Czestochowa was also famous for the printing presses of Samuel and Wilhelm Kohn and the Oderfeld brothers, which existed until the German occupation in 1940 and 1941, respectively. In addition, a number of Jewish newspapers were in circulation—*Hajn*, among them, which lasted until the war.

Thirty thousand of the town's Jews perished in WWII, mainly in Treblinka. Today, there are hardly any traces left of that community.

A Polish and Hebrew plaque at Kawia 20–21 commemorates the Jews shot during the liquidation of the ghetto on September 24, 1942.

A mass grave and a monument at the Jewish cemetery at the end of Ulica Zlota honors the town's Jewish victims, as well as the members of the Jewish Fighting Organization (Z.O.B.).

During January 1943, an armed resistance occurred under the leadership of Mendel Fiszelewicz. Miraculously, 5,200 Jews working in the Hasag plant were saved when the Red Army entered the area.

A few famous Jewish citizens of Czestochowa include Henryk Merkusfeld, a philanthropist; Jan Glickson, a lawyer; and Edward Kohn, a doctor.

Czyzew-Osada

A completely destroyed cemetery lies in the town, whose synagogue at Piwna is currently a private residence.

D

Dabrowa

The town's former synagogue is now a warehouse.

Dabrowa Bialostocka

A nineteenth-century Jewish cemetery is located at Wyzwolenia.

Dabrowa Tarnowska

The Jewish community here dates back to the seventeenth century. By 1939, the town was home to approximately 2,500 Jewish citizens—or 40% of its total population. It was liquidated by deportation to the ghetto of Tarnow, as well as to the death camp at Belzec.

The majority of Jewish interest sites are located on Ulica Berka Joselewicza. They include the synagogue, built in the nineteenth century by Abraham Goldstein, and now used as a cultural center; a cemetery that contains 50 matzevot; two monuments that honor the victims of Shoah; and the "Talmud-Tora" school, which now serves as an office building.

Dabrowno

The former synagogue is presently used as a warehouse.

Debica (Dembitz)—west of Rzeszow

The synagogue at Krakowska 3 is currently a warehouse. Located at Cmentarna, the cemetery possesses 50 remaining matzevot. A memorial in the woods of Wolica commemorates the 600 Jews of Debica shot by the Germans on July 10, 1942.

Deblin—northwest of Lublin

An obelisk commemorates the victims of this branch of the Majdanek concentration camp, where slave laborers worked at the Heinkel Aeroplane Works.

Drobin—northwest of Plonsk

A memorial at the Jewish cemetery (Ulica Sierpecka 54) honors the victims of the Holocaust.

Drohiczyn

The town is famous for the historical document issued by the Grand Duke Witold of Lithuania that granted Jews the right to settle in the town.

Dukla—southeast of Cracow

The former synagogue currently houses a market, while Baron Hirsch's school at "Bursa Zydowska" now serves as a public school.

Dubienko

A mass grave at the Jewish cemetery holds the remains of 150 Jews who were murdered between 1942 and 1943.

Dzierzoniow—north of Klodzko

A congregation and a house of worship are located at Krasickiego 28. The Jewish cemetery, at Wolna 6, contains approximately 100 matzevot.

Dzwierzno

A mass grave at the cemetery contains the remains of some 1,000 Jewish women who were prisoners at Bocienie and Szerakopas.

G

Gdansk (Danzig)

The Jewish presence here dates back to the fourteenth century, notwithstanding the restrictions imposed on Jews by the Teutonic Knights and subsequent Polish kings and city councils. Jewish settlements were definitely established in the city's neighboring villages—Stare Szkozy, Chmielniki, and Winnica. There is even a record of a kosher inn, the Zloty Pierscien-Gold Ring.

Today there exists but remnants of the cemetery at Zydowskie Gorki (Jewish Hills). The great synagogue at Ujezdzalnia (now Boguslawskiego) was demolished by the Nazis in 1939, while the surviving synagogue buildings are now home to different institutions: Biskupia Gora at Menowitz 2 serves as a Pentecostal Church, and Wrzeszcz at Partyzantow 7 houses a music school.

The Jewish cemetery between Reformacka, Cmentarna, and Browicza streets contains 100 matzevot, the oldest of which dates back to 1786.

The most significant testimonies to the Jewish presence in Gdansk, however, are the paintings by Izaak Van Den Blocke that adorn City Hall. They treat biblical scenes, in addition to the participation of Jewish merchants in the city's commerce.

Gielczyn

A monument in the woods outside the town honors 12,000 people executed by the Germans from mid-1942 to September 1944. Of those murdered, 7,000 were Jewish.

Gizycko

The town's Jewish cemetery at Warszawska Street was completely destroyed.

Gliniska

A grave here holds a number of Jewish families murdered on October 30, 1942.

Gliwice—west of Katowice

A part of Germany before WWII, Gliwice suffered from Nazi excesses as early as the opening years of the 1930s. All the Jewish men of the area were deported to Buchenwald in 1938.

The cemetery at Na Piasku holds 800 matzevot, while the cemetery at Poniatiowskiego contains 400. A tablet at Przszynski 204 commemorates the victims of a nearby camp.

The house of worship and congregation is at Dolne Waly 9, while the former synagogue at Dolne Waly 15 sits deserted.

Glogow Malopolski—west of Rzeszow

Three mass graves near the road to Rzeszow mark the spot where the Jews of Rzeszow were shot during the liquidation of the ghetto.

Goldap

The cemetery at Cmentarna still holds a few matzevot.

Golub-Dobrzyn

A monument at Plac Stulecia honors the citizens and Jewish population who lost their lives during the war. Both the cemeteries at Krasickiego and at Rypinska were completely destroyed.

Gora Kalwaria (Gur-Ger)—near Warsaw

Jews were permitted to settle in this town in 1745. By the eve of WWII, half of the town's population—or 3,500 of its citizens—were Jewish. Thus was Gora Kalwaria known as "New Jerusalem."

Still standing is Gerer Rebbe's synagogue at Pijarska, once the seat of the famous Hassidic dynasty of the Alter family, though it now serves as a warehouse and barn. The only remnant of the building's Jewish history is the metal framework of a Magen David.

What was once the residence of the Gerer Rebbe and the adjacent yeshiva have been converted into tenements. He managed to escape from Poland, and reached Palestine in 1940.

In the old Jewish cemetery at Kalwaryjska, there stands a monument to the 5,000 Jews who perished in the town at the hands of the Nazis.

Gorlice (Gorlitza)—west of Krasno

At Ulica Korczaka (named in honor of Janusz Korczak), a tablet marks the location of the camp where the liquidation of the Gorlice Ghetto took place. Though a memorial tablet is set into its walls, the former synagogue at Piekarska 3 now houses a bakery. The synagogue at Dworzysko is now a fire station.

Grajewo

The town's former synagogue has been renovated to serve as a cultural center.

Grodno

A monument here remembers Jewish women from Hungary, Romania, and Bulgaria who worked at fortifications in what was a branch of Stutthof. This camp existed from August 1944 to January 1945.

Grojec—south of Warsaw

By 1856, nearly 70% of Grojec's citizens were Jewish. By 1939, the Jewish population had reached 5,200 individuals. A ghetto was created in July 1940. Many of its inhabitants were herded into the Warsaw Ghetto, while the remaining 3,000 were sent to Treblinka.

A cemetery near the road to Mszonowa marks the mass grave of extermination victims who were killed in 1943. A rabbi's house adjacent to the cemetery once served as a community house; the property is now a private residence.

Gross-Rosen (Rogoznica)—near Wroclaw

The concentration camp located at Kamienna Gora was a branch of Sachsenhausen, which initially held Soviet POWs. In May 1941, it became the independent camp of Gross-Rosen. Towards the latter part of 1945, it contained some 84,000 prisoners; but at various times throughout the war, it held as many as 125,000 captives.

Some original structures have been reconstructed and turned into a museum. Some 40,000 victims in all were murdered there. In honor of these victims stands a monument and mausoleum constructed of granite stones excavated by the prisoners. The wall contains earth from the different branches of the camp.

PLAN OF CONCENTRATION CAMP AT GROSS-ROSEN

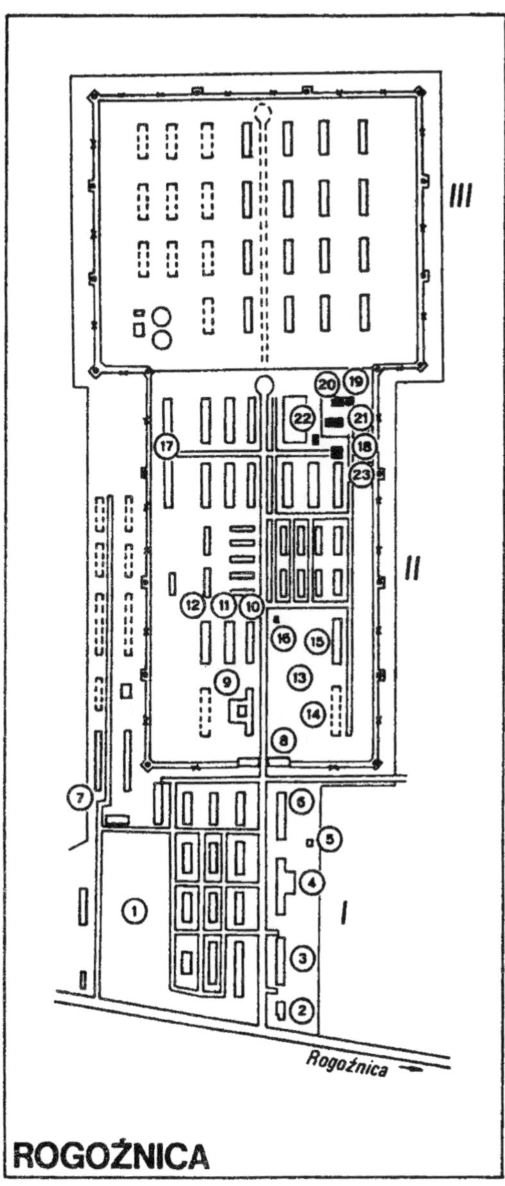

I. COMMANDANT'S BUILDING

1. Barracks of S.S.
2. Prison
3. Commandant's office
4. S.S. Canteen (presently holding the Museum)
5. Dog house
6. Block Fuhrer (Head of the Block)
7. Stores and workshops

II. MAIN CAMP

8. Main gate
9. Admittance office
10. Clothing stores
11. Old baths
12. Storage depots
13. Parade grounds
14. Laundry
15. Kitchen
16. Bell tower
17. Hospital
18. Place of execution
19. Old crematorium
20. Gas chamber
21. Crematorium

H

Halbow (Krempna Parish)

A mass grave here holds the remains of 1,257 Jews from the area and those brought from Lodz.

Hrubieszow (Rubishow)—southeast of Lublin

At the Jewish cemetery at Ulica Krucza stands a monument in memory of the 5,700 inhabitants—or 10,000 total, including local Jews—of the open ghetto here. The ghetto was liquidated in 1942, and its inhabitants deported to Sobibor.

An underground organization was established here in 1941 under the command of Arieh Perec (Porecki) and Solomon Brand.

I

Ilawa—west of Olsztyn

At the steam engine factory (Lokomotywnia PKP) at Ulica Wojska Polskiego 9, a plaque marks the location of a local penal work camp. The cemetery at Biskupia was completely devastated.

Ilowa—near Bialoslawiec

A memorial tablet here is dedicated to the prisoners of the slave labor camp, which was a sub-branch of Gross-Rosen.

Inowroclaw—south of Bydgoszez

The first mention of a Jewish presence here dates back to 1447. At Ulica Okrezek, a memorial erected in 1975 commemorates victims of the concentration camp at Blonie. The cemetery at Studzienna was completely destroyed.

Izbica—near Zamosc

Tzadik Mordechai Joseph Leiner held his court here, where his son and successor, Yaacov Leiner, wrote *Beth Yaacov*.

Four thousand Jews lived in Izbica just before the outbreak of war. The town subsequently served as a transit point to Belzec and Sobibor for Czech, Austrian, and German Jews, as well as for local Jews. The town's last Jewish citizens were deported in 1943 to various death camps.

The Germans executed more than 4,000 Jews in Izbica, and buried them in mass graves. Though the Jewish cemetery was nearly destroyed, graves of ghetto victims killed in 1941 still exist.

J

Jagiella-Niechcialki—south of Sienawa

A monument here commemorates the victims of two nearby camps: Perlkinie and Wolce Pelkinskie. About 8,000 persons— predominantly Jews, Gypsies, and Russian POWs—are buried in the town.

Janikowo

A mass grave at the Catholic cemetery contains Jews whose remains were discovered near railroad tracks at Inowroclaw-Poznan.

Janow

Established in the eighteenth century, the town's Jewish cemetery still holds 250 matzevot.

Janowo

The Jewish cemetery here possesses ten remaining matzevot.

Janow Podlaski

The town is home to a destroyed cemetery at Bialska.

Jaroslaw—east of Cracow

Built in 1807, the synagogue at Opolska 2 now houses an art school.

Jasionowka

A memorial tablet marks the mass grave of 300 Jews who were executed by the Germans. In addition to this mass grave, the nineteenth-century cemetery contains 400 matzevot.

Jaslo

In the Krajowicki Forest, a memorial tablet stands at the mass grave of 260 victims shot by the Nazis in July 1942. The cemetery at Florianska contains 100 matzevot, while the former synagogue now serves as a restaurant.

Jedwabne

Under Soviet occupation from September 1939 until June 1941 when the Germans attacked the Soviet Union, Jedwabne was the scene of a mass murder of 1,600 Jews on July 10, 1941. Originally attributed to the German Einsatztruppen, which carried out many mass execution in the area, this crime was in fact carried out by the local population, according to a book by Prof. Jan Tomasz Gross entitled *The Neighbors* (2000). The Polish government is investigating the massacre.

Jozefow—south of Lublin

An obelisk erected in 1974 stands at the execution spot of Jews from Poland, Czechoslovakia, and Austria.

The town's former synagogue now serves as a silo.

K

Katowice—west of Cracow

Though a number of Jews emigrated following the 1937 pogrom, the town's Jewish community still contained 8,500 members before the war. Most of these remaining individuals were forcibly evacuated during the first few months of the German occupation.

A monument stands at the former location of the German-destroyed synagogue—between Mickiewicza and Skargi Streets—which has been replaced by an apartment building. The Jewish community center and house of worship is at Mlynska 13.

Kazimierz-upon-Vistula (Kazimierz Dolny / Kuzmir)

Throughout the fifteenth and sixteenth centuries, Kazimierz-upon-Vistula housed regional markets from the greater Lublin area. Beginning in the nineteenth century, the town's population became predominantly Jewish; by March 1942, no Jews remained in the town.

An early eighteenth-century synagogue on Lubelska now serves as a "Wisla" cinema, though a memorial tablet marks the building's heritage.

A monument at the cemetery consists of broken gravestones that create a "wailing wall" for Holocaust victims. A stone memorial erected by Arie Meler of Canada marks a mass grave in the Jewish cemetery; it commemorates his parents along with 500 other local Jews who were murdered in October 1942. While the cemetery at Lubelska was completely destroyed, the cemetery at Czerniawa possesses a few matzevot and a monument. A small collection of Judaica is exhibited at the Gold Museum.

Incidentally, Kazimierz is the birthplace of S.L. Szneiderman, who wrote under the pseudonym A. Lubliner;

Memorial-Lapidarium made of tombstones, Kazimierz-upon-Vistula.

and a small inn here is named Esterka in honor of King Kazimierz's supposedly Jewish wife, Esther.

Kielce (Keltz)—north of Cracow

Kielce is a provincial capital in south-central Poland. On the eve of WWII, 40% of its 50,000 citizens were Jewish. The ghetto was established in 1941, and existed until May 1943. Used as an archive today, the former synagogue stands at Rewolucji Pazdziernikowej. The cemetery at Pakosz Dolny holds approximately 150 matzevot.

Dawidek Rubinowicz, author of *The Diary of Dawidek Rubinowicz*, was born here in 1927. He perished at Treblinka on September 22, 1942. His diary was first published in Polish 18 years later.

Following the conclusion of the war, Kielce was also the site of sporadic and deadly anti-Jewish activities. According to a report by the Manchester Guardian, 350 Jews were killed in post-war 1945. Forty-two Jews who had survived the war were murdered one year later, during the infamous pogrom that triggered the emigration of some 20,000 Jews to Palestine.

A monument has recently been erected at Planty 7 in honor of these post-war victims.

Kieszczele

A nineteenth-century Jewish cemetery remains here with 250 matzevot.

Kock—north of Lublin

The first Jews immigrated here in the seventeenth century. Tzadik Mendel of Kock (Menachem Mendel Morgenstern) settled in the town in 1829, heading an important Hassidic school. In fact, he was a teacher of the famous Gerer Rebbe (see Gora Kalwaria).

Ulica Berka Joselewicza was named after Colonel Berek Joselewicz, commander of the Jewish Legion, who fell in the Battle at Kock while fighting in the anti-Russian rebellion of General Tadeusz Kosciuszko.

The Jewish community of Kock numbered 2,500 before WWII. Most of them were murdered at Parczew in August 1942.

The cemetery is nearly destroyed, with only a few matzevot remaining.

Kokoszki—near Gdansk

This town served as a branch of the Stutthof Concentration Camp. A pillar commemorates the victims of the camp, which was liberated by the Red Army on March 26, 1945.

Kolaki Koscielne

A memorial stone near the railroad station marks the spot of the execution of 1,000 Jews from Rutek and Zambrowo in September 1941.

Kolbuszowa—north of Rzeszow

Built in 1860, the synagogue at Piekarska was a wheat silo for a number of years, and now serves as a museum. The cemetery at Krakowska contains mass graves.

Kolce

In the fall of 1943, the Germans formed a forced labor camp for Jews from Poland, Hungary, and Greece. It was transformed into a subcamp of Gross-Rosen in June 1944, before being liberated the following May 8–9 by the Red Army.

A Jewish cemetery contains 25 mass graves. Tablets in Hebrew and Polish stand at the cemetery gate.

Kolno

The eighteenth-century synagogue at Strazacka has been rebuilt for use as a store. Established in 1817, the Jewish cemetery at Aleksandrowska features 100 matzevot.

Kolo—south of Tomaszow Mazowiecki

On the remains of the synagogue and Mikva burned down in 1939, a stone stands in commemoration of Jews who perished in neighboring camps.

Konin—south of Inowroclaw

A tablet at the intersection of Bydgoska and Kolejowa honors a few hundred victims of the nearby labor camp.

Remnants of a synagogue are also to be seen here.

Koniusz

A memorial stone at the parish cemetery honors a Polish family of seven (including three children) that was shot on June 22, 1943 for illegally hiding Jews.

Kornick

A nineteenth-century Moorish synagogue is located here.

Kosarzyska (Piwniczna County)—south of Nowy Sacz

A plaque here commemorates 19 Poles executed on September 3, 1943 for aiding Jews.

Kozienice

This town was a Hassidic center led by Rabbi Israel Ben Shabtai Hapstein, better known as "The Great Magician," who was also a famous Talmudist.

Krasnik—south of Lublin

Established in 1637 at Boznicza, the synagogue currently houses city offices. The cemetery at Podwalna was rebuilt after its wartime destruction; while the cemetery at Gory still possesses a few fragile matzevot. A memorial at what was known as Bieruta honors the victims of the local labor camp, which was a branch of Majdanek.

Krepa

A grave at the parish cemetery commemorates a Jew and the Polish villager who hid him—both of whom were shot by the Germans in September 1944.

Krepice (Melgiew County)

A memorial here honors the victims of mass executions that were carried out in the woods of Krepiec between 1941 and 1944. A total of 30,000 people from Lublin and Majdanek were shot there—Jews, Poles, and Russians, among them.

Krosniewice (Kroshnivits)—south of Wroclawek

The synagogue now serves as a cinema.

Krosno—south of Rzeszow

Jews arrived in Krosno in the fifteenth century. Before the war, it had a well-established community of 2,500 members and important social institutions: a loan association and a charitable organization, among many others.

Most of the town's Jews perished in Belzec in 1942. The cemetery at Ulica Okrzej has 100 remaining matzevot, as well as a mass grave of Shoah victims.

Krynki—east of Bialystok

The Jewish presence here dates back to the seventeenth century. On the eve of WWII, the Jewish community numbered 3,500—a population served by a number of schools and sports clubs.

The Germans arrived in Krynki in 1941, after the invasion of the USSR. The deportation to Auschwitz occurred in July 1943.

The synagogue at Bialostocka now houses a cinema. The Jewish cemetery contains 3,000 graves, the oldest of which dates back to 1750.

Krzeszow—west of Cracow

A memorial erected by Charles Schreiber of New York honors the 1,500 Jews of Krzeszow who were murdered in a nearby forest. The cemetery has 50 matzevot remaining, the oldest of which dates back to 1852.

Krzyszyn

An abandoned synagogue sits at Grodzienska. The Jewish cemetery possesses 200 matzevot.

Kudowa Zdroj—south of Walbrzych

At St. Catherine Church (Sw. Katarzyny), a mass grave notes victims of the sub-branch of Gross-Rosen-Sackisch that held Jewish girls from Poland, Czechoslovakia, and Hungary.

There was also a nearby branch of the Stutthof Concentration Camp. An obelisk commemorates the victims of the camp, which was liberated by the Red Army on March 26, 1945.

Kutery—south of Plonsk

A monument to the soldiers of the People's Guard led by Stanislaw Olczyk stands here. His partisans and a number of Jewish families were killed in a skirmish with German troops on December 6, 1942.

Kutno

The Jewish community of Kutno dates back to the fifteenth century. The town was renowned as a Tora study center, as well as a center of the Haskalah Movement. Nine thousand Jews lived in Kutno before the war. Most of them perished in Chelmno after the ghetto was liquidated in March 1942.

The synagogue is now an office. Established in 1793, the cemetery at Spokojna now has but a few dozen remaining matzevot.

L

Lancut—east of Rzeszow

The Jewish presence in this southeastern town can be traced back to the sixteenth century. In the 1930s, as a result of the depression and an economic boycott, Jews were in dire need of, and to some extent existed on, foreign Jewish aid. On the brink of WWII, Jews comprised some 40% of the town's population (2,800 persons). Not a single one was left by August 1, 1942.

The Lancut synagogue, a masonry building built in 1761 just outside the grounds of Count Potocki's residence, survived the war. Thereafter, Dr. Stanislaw Balicki convinced the town council to spare the building and to create a provincial museum to celebrate Lancut's six-hundreth anniversary.

Dr. Balicki wanted to commemorate his murdered Jewish friends—a goal that was realized in 1981 with the building's restoration as a museum. It is also used for official ceremonies during the Lancut Festival.

A tablet at the Jewish cemetery at Ulica Traugutta commemorates the Jews of the town. There are no matzevot left.

Synagogue in Lancut.

The famous rabbis of Lancut include Moshe Hirsh Melizlich, Moshe Ben Itzhak Eisik, and Yaacov Horowitz.

Lask

The Jewish community was established here in the sixteenth century, and became an important center of Jewish studies. The town's famous rabbis include Meir Goertz, Moshe Yehuda Lejb, and Pinchas Zelig.

There were nearly 4,000 Jews in Lask before the war erupted. The ghetto was established in November 1940, and its liquidation occurred in 1942 by deportation to Chelmno.

The former synagogue now houses a fire station. The cemetery at Ulica Mickiewicza was destroyed during the war, while only 80 matzevot have survived in the cemetery at Lopatki.

Laslo

A memorial plaque at the Jewish cemetery at Ulica Florjanska honors the victims of the Laslo Ghetto.

Lasy Kazimierzowskie

A monument here honors the 8,000 Jewish victims who were executed in the woods in October 1941. (See *Zagorow*.)

Leczna (Lentchna)—near Lublin

The first recorded mention of Jews here dates back to 1501. Before the war, the Jewish community numbered 2,300 persons.

A tablet commemorates the victims of the ghetto, which also held some Slovak and Czech Jews. At the time of its liquidation in September 1943, 1,000 inhabitants were immediately shot. Those remaining were deported to Sobibor.

The synagogue at Ulica Boznicza 19 (Synagogue Street) was constructed in 1648. It was rebuilt in the 1950s and now serves as a Judaica museum. A tablet on one of the building's walls honors 1,046 Jews shot between 1940 and 1942. The cemetery near the highway is almost completely destroyed.

Legnica—west of Wroclaw

The Jewish presence here can be traced back to 1301. The Nazi pogrom of 1938 left the town with a mere 200 Jews who were subsequently deported to Terezin in June of 1941.

Established in 1837, the cemetery at Wroclawska now consists of approximately 1,000 graves. A memorial honoring the heroes of the Warsaw Ghetto was erected at Plac

Bohaterow Getta to coincide with the twentieth anniversary of that Uprising.

The current congregation and synagogue is at Chojnowska 17.

Lekawica

A common grave at the parish cemetery notes three Jews and the Pole who hid them. The Germans executed them all in 1941.

Lelow (Lelowo)

This town is the birthplace of a Hassidic dynasty founded by David Ben Salomon of Lelow—a dynasty that continues today in Israel.

Lesko—southeast of Cracow

The Jewish community was exterminated in August 1941 in Zaslawie. A grave of Holocaust victims lies at the Jewish cemetery, which contains 2,000 well-preserved tombs, some dating back to the sixteenth century.

A restored seventeenth-century synagogue stands on Moniuszki and presently serves as a regional museum.

Synagogue in Lesko.

Lesno

An obelisk and commemorative tablets honor 64 Jewish women who were shot by the Germans in 1945.

Lezachow-Glazyna

A stone marks the place where 16 people—six Jews among them—were executed by the Gestapo and the Ukrainian police on August 29, 1941.

Lezajsk—north of Rzeszow

This town was the seat of a Hassidic dynasty headed by Rabbi Elimelech of Lezajsk, better known as Rabbi Lizensker.

Lobez-Swietobrzec

A stone has been placed in memory of Lieutenant Alexander Segal, who was killed in action against retreating Germans.

Lodz

See Chapter Five, page 147.

Lomazy—south of Biala Podlaska

Here lies a mass grave containing 2,000 Jews who were murdered during the liquidation of the town's ghetto.

Lomza—west of Bialystok

At the beginning of the nineteenth century, there were 737 Jews in Lomza. The community was served by a synagogue, two Yeshivot, and two newspapers: *Lomsher Shtyme* and *Lomsher Lebn*. Agudat Israel and Bund were also active in town.

By 1939 the Jewish population had grown to 11,000. The ghetto was established on August 12, 1941 and was liquidated the following November by deportation to Auschwitz.

A memorial stone at Ulica Zambrowska marks the mass grave of German execution victims from 1941 to 1943.

Established in the nineteenth century, the cemeteries at Ulica Rybki and Waska 69 each contain over 150 matzevot. An obelisk at the latter cemetery commemorates the victims of mass murder between 1941 and 1943.

A memorial tablet at the location of a synagogue burned by the Germans in September of 1939 honors over 9,000 of the town's Jewish citizens.

Losice

A destroyed Jewish cemetery here now serves as a public park.

Lowicz

Before the war, the Jewish population of the town was 45,000. It boasted a synagogue, a cemetery, and a weekly newspaper—*Mazowsher Wochenblat*. The inhabitants of the ghetto were deported to the Warsaw Ghetto.

The cemetery at Leczycka was established in 1830 and still possesses 200 matzevot.

Built in 1897, the synagogue at Browarna 10 now houses municipal offices.

Lubaczow—south of Tomaszow Lubelski

Jews first immigrated here in 1498. Before Baron Edmund de Rothschild funded the reconstruction of the synagogue in 1899, the town played host to a number of famous rabbis: Hersh Elimelech and Shmuel Nachum Gassenbauer, among them.

Most of the 2,500-strong Jewish community perished in Sobibor and Belzec.

A number of Jewish partisan units fought in the area under the command of Mietek Gruber and Samuel Jegier.

The former synagogue now serves as a warehouse.

Lublin

See Chapter Five, page 153.

Lubon—south of Lawice

A monument stands at the location of a labor camp for Jews who were forced to work on the Berlin-Warsaw railway (1941–1943).

Lutowisko—south of Przemysl

A memorial erected in 1969 commemorates 650 Jews and Gypsies who were shot near the Catholic Church in 1943. The Jewish cemetery contains some 400 graves.

M

Majdanek (Lublin)

The Majdanek Concentration Camp was established in November 1941. Within its confines between 120,000 and 200,000 Jews from the ghettos of Warsaw and Lublin perished. Nineteen thousand of these victims were shot on November 3, 1943—a crime euphemistically referred to by the Germans as *Ernfest*, or harvest.

Today, the Polish government preserves the camp as a monument in which the barracks and gas chambers are still to be seen. At the camp's entrance stands a huge monument in the form of a gate that was designed by Viktor Tolkin and Janusz Dembek to subtly suggest a menorah. A memorial on the site is comprised of a huge mound of ashes and bones from the victims.

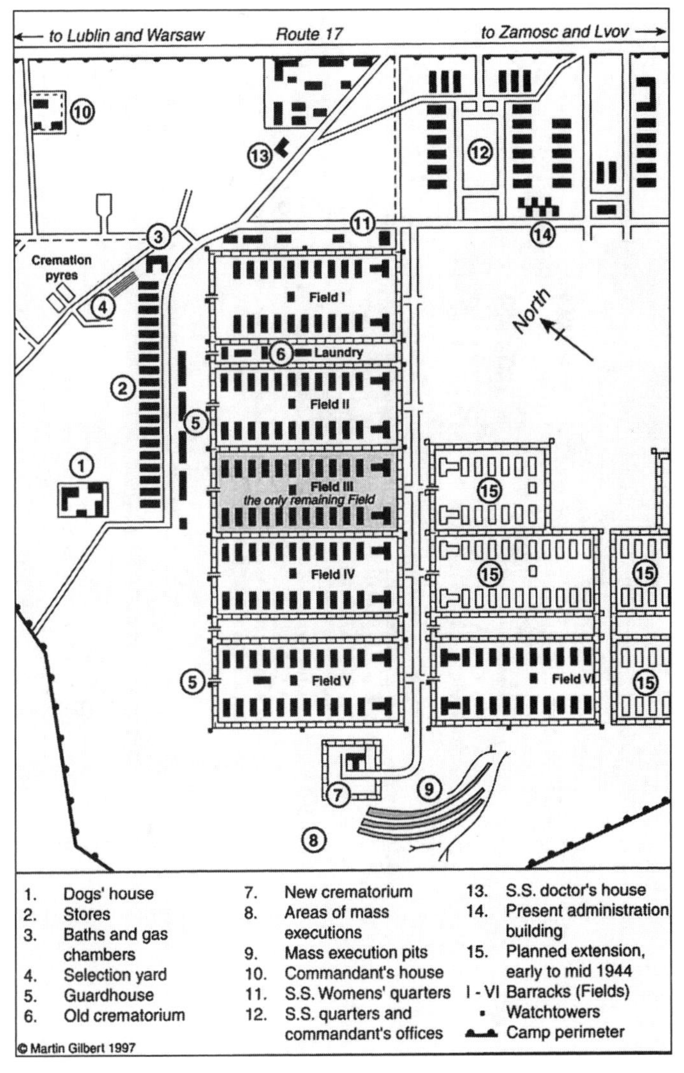

Majdanek. Courtesy of Martin Gilbert.

Majdanek Monument, designed by W. Tolkin and J. Dembek.

Makow Mazowiecki—north of Warsaw

The Jewish community here dates back to the middle of the sixteenth century, and by 1827, it comprised 90% of the town's total population.

On the eve of WWII, there were 3,500 Jewish citizens of Makow. The Germans established the ghetto in September 1941. At the end of the following year, its inhabitants were deported to Treblinka.

A monument to Holocaust victims was erected in 1987 using broken matzevot from the grounds of a destroyed cemetery near the railroad station. Broken matzevot were also used to construct a memorial erected on the site of the Jewish cemetery in 1947.

The synagogue at Zielony Rynek 5 was devastated and then rebuilt after the war for use as an apartment building. The former mikva at Ulica Przasnyska 19 now serves as a garage.

Malki

A monument here honors local Jewish women murdered in January 1945.

Miedzyrzec—west of Biala Podlaska

The town's neo-classical nineteenth-century synagogue at Piotra Skargi Cemetery (at Waszkiewicza) was completely destroyed during the war.

Miedzyrzec Podlaski—west of Biala Podlaska

The Jewish presence was established here by the sixteenth century and was served by a pre-war synagogue and a number of houses of worship.

A memorial at the Jewish cemetery at Ulica Brzeska 60 commemorates 10,000 Jews from the area.

Mielec-Borek (Melitz)—south of Sandomierz

At the Jewish cemetery at Ulica Traugutta, an obelisk commemorates 1,000 local Jews who were shot on March 9, 1942, during the liquidation of the ghetto.

A monument in the town square stands on the spot where the Germans burned down the synagogue and the worshippers inside of it.

Mielnik

The town's nineteenth-century synagogue now serves as the seat of the local council. The Jewish cemetery contains 50 matzevot.

Minsk Mazowiecki (Novomintz)—west of Siedlce

Jews first settled here in the early part of the nineteenth century, and the town soon became a stronghold of the Hassidic Movement, known for the court of Tzadik Yaacov Perlow.

The Jewish community of Minsk numbered nearly 6,000 before the war. The ghetto was established in 1940, and also imprisoned Jews from Lipno, Pabianice, and Kalisz. After mass executions on August 21, 1942, the remaining inhabitants of the ghetto were deported to Treblinka.

At the school building on Ulica Siennicka, a commemorative tablet honors the 200 victims who perished when Germans burned the building.

A monument honoring 5,500 local Holocaust victims was erected in 1965 on the grounds of the Jewish cemetery on Ulica Dabrowska.

Morag

The town's Jewish cemetery contains but a few remaining matzevot.

Msciwuje

In a neighboring forest, a memorial stone marks the mass grave of some 4,000 Jews from Lomza who were murdered in 1941–1942.

Myslenice—near Cracow

At the Jewish cemetery on Ulica Tasnowa, an obelisk commemorates local Jews who were deported to the death camps on August 22, 1942.

N

Nekla

An obelisk at the railroad tracks from Nekla to Giecz marks the location of the Julag (Jewish camp), whose laborers were forced to work on the Poznan-Warsaw railroad. A mass grave containing the remains of 180 Jews lies in the Catholic cemetery.

Nielisz—west of Zamosc

At the exact spot where 39 Jews were murdered, a memorial honors victims of the German terror in 1943.

Niskie Brodno

An obelisk at Lake Niskie Brodno (near Brodnica) honors Jewish women who worked and perished in the nearby camp. Their remains were exhumed from mass graves after the war and interred at the Military Cemetery of Bydgoszcz.

Nowa Huta—east of Cracow

The Youth Culture House at Osiedle Zgody 13 has a plaque that commemorates Janusz Korczak.

Nowa Wies—south of Tarnobrzeg

An obelisk in the woods near the road to Zapole marks the spot where 250 Jews were executed in 1942. Nine years later, the bodies were transferred to the Jewish cemetery in Kolbuszowa.

Nowy Sacz (Neisantz)—southeast of Cracow

The first mention of Jews here dates back to 1409. In the nineteenth century, Tzadik Chaim Ben Arieh Lejb Halberstam held his court in town. On the eve of WWII, there were approximately 150,000 Jews in Nowy Sacz and its suburbs. The ghetto was established in August 1941. One year later, its occupants were deported to Belzec.

At the Jewish cemetery at Ulica Rybacka, a plaque indicates the sites of mass executions and honors the 25,000 people buried there. An abandoned synagogue also survives in Nowy Sacz.

Nowy Targ (Neumarkt)—south of Cracow

There is a commemorative tablet at the Jewish cemetery at Ulica Strzelnicza, where 2,900 local Jews were executed. The house of worship at Szaflarska 19 now houses a mechanic's shop.

Nowy Wisnicz—west of Limanowa

At the invitation of Count Ludomirski, Jews settled here in 1606. The 1,000 members of the Jewish community were deported to Belzec in the summer of 1942.

The cemetery near the road to Limanowa features approximately 300 matzevot. It was cleaned, restored, and fenced in the 1980s.

O

Olsztyn—north of Warsaw

The Jewish community here dates back to the latter part of the eighteenth century. Erich Mendelson, the renowned architect, was born in town at Staromiejska 8.

As the town was part of the Third Reich before the war, the persecution of Jews began in the early 1930s. The Yellow Star was introduced in 1938.

The cemetery at Zyndrama z Maszkowic is destroyed, and the area now serves as a park. At Kollataja 16, the synagogue is now a residence.

Opoczno—southwest of Warsaw

The history of Jews here begins in the reign of Casimir the Great, whose supposed love for Esterka led to a legend that her house was located in this town.

The ghetto established in 1940 was liquidated in 1942 with the deportation of its inhabitants to Treblinka. A Jewish partisan unit fought in the neighboring forest under the command of Kaniowski (Julian Ajzenman).

A mass grave contains Jews who were shot by the German at the military cemetery in 1943, and exhumed in June 1967.

The eighteenth-century synagogue currently houses a cinema.

Orla—south of Bielsk Podlaski

The town's eighteenth-century synagogue now serves as a warehouse.

Osowa

A memorial here commemorates the inmates of the labor camp established in 1941. The camp was liquidated in 1943, and its inmates were deported to Sobibor.

Ostroda

The town's Jewish cemetery at Armii Ludowej possesses but two remaining matzevot.

Ostroleka—north of Warsaw

Most of the local Jews were deportated by the Germans to the Soviet-occupied part of Poland in 1939.

The cemetery at Stefczyka is completely destroyed. The former synagogue is now a garage.

Ostrowiec Swietokrzyski—south of Chotnice

The Jewish community here dates back to the seventeenth century. By the outbreak of WWII, 50% of the town's population was Jewish. The last of this group were deported to Auschwitz on August 3, 1944.

A resistance group was active in the ghetto under the leadership of David Kempinski, Moshe Stein, and the Kopel brothers.

The cemetery at Sienkiewicza contains some 200 gravestones including that of Tzadik Meier Halewi Halsztok.

Ostrow Mazowiecki—near Bialystok

The Germans deported the bulk of local Jews to the Soviet-occupied part of Poland in 1939. The local Jewish cemetery at Broniewskiego was completely destroyed.

In the woods near Ostrow Mazowiecki-Wyszkow Road, a marker notes the murder of 600 Jews on September 11, 1939.

Oswiecim (Oshpitzin)—west of Cracow

The first Jews arrived here in 1564. By the outbreak of WWII, 33% of Oswiecim's citizens were Jewish—or 4,000 out of 12,000.

The Jewish cemetery between Dabrowskiego and Wysokie Brzegi Streets contains 1,000 graves. It was restored in 1980.

The synagogue at Berka Joselewicza is currently used as a residence, while plans for the restoration of Lomdei Mishnayot Synagogue are progressing.

A Cultural Foundation has recently been established under the auspices of the Auschwitz Jewish Center Foundation of New York. It will be located at the Habersfeld House and will show the history of Jewish life in Oswiecim before the war.

Otwock—south of Warsaw

A monument marks the spot where the Germans shot 1,500 Jews from the local ghetto on August 19–20, 1942.

The town's new Jewish cemetery with 200 gravestones is in an extremely dilapidated state.

Ozarow

The town is home to a Jewish cemetery.

P

Palmiry—northwest of Warsaw

In the woods of Kampinow near Warsaw (see page 90), a mass grave cum cemetery memorializes the spot where 1,700 people were executed in January 1940. At least 250 of those murdered were Jewish.

Parczew (Partzeva)—west of Warsaw

A Jewish partisan unit under the command of Alexander Skotnicki was formed here among Jews who managed to escape from a Treblinka-bound train.

At the municipal park, a memorial commemorates 100 Jewish POWs shot by the Germans on September 18, 1939.

The synagogue at Piwonia now houses a cinema, while the synagogue at Zabia currently serves as a kindergarten. The Jewish cemetery is completely destroyed.

Pieszyce—south of Olawa

Near the road to Dzierzoniowa, a stone commemorates the Warsaw Ghetto Uprising. It was unveiled to coincide with the twentieth anniversary of the uprising.

Inscribed in both Polish and Yiddish, a monument stands at the Langenbielan I branch of Gross-Rosen. The branch held 1,500 prisoners, almost all of them Jews from Hungary and Slovakia. The camp was liberated on May 8, 1945.

The Woods of Kampinow

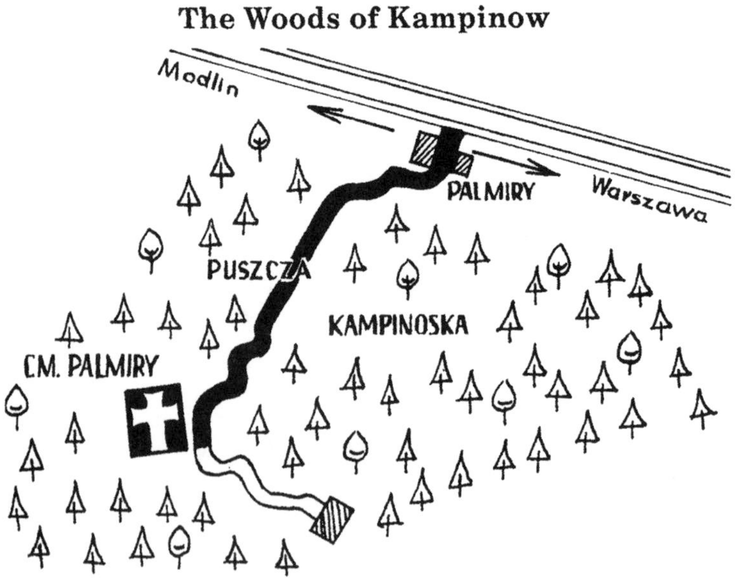

Pietkowiec (Wadowice Gorne Parish)

A tablet on the local school building marks the spot where a family of five was murdered.

Pilzno—north of Taslo

The Jewish community was established here in the sixteenth century. There were approximately 3,500 local Jews on the eve of WWII. During the deportation to Treblinka in August 1942, some Jews escaped to neighboring forests and formed partisan units under the command of Zalman Fajnsztat and Michal Majtek.

A grave at the parish cemetery is for Jan Bobowski, who was murdered by the Germans on April 24, 1943 for assisting Jews. At the Jewish cemetery at Skarpy, a monument honors murdered Jews from the greater Pilzno region.

Pinczow—north of Cracow

At Ulica Klasztorna stands a sixteenth-century Renaissance synagogue that is currently being renovated for possible use as a museum.

The cemeteries at both Batalionow Chlopskich and Slabska are completely destroyed.

Piotrkow Trybunalski (Petrikov)—south of Lodz

The Jewish community here dates back to the sixteenth century. King Jan Sobieski III, hero of the Battle of Vienna, reaffirmed the Jews' right to settle in Piotrkow in 1679. Before the outbreak of WWII, the Jewish population exceeded 10,000.

The local labor camps were liquidated in November 1944, and the survivors were deported to Ravensbruck and Buchenwald, as well as to ammuntion factories in Czechoslovakia.

The Jewish cemetery at Spacerowa was devastated by the Germans, who used its grounds for the mass executions of ghetto inhabitants—the best known of which occurred on August 14, 1942. A symbolic grave commemorates these victims. The cemetery at Wojska Polskiego was also entirely destroyed.

The "Duza" (Big) Synagogue was rebuilt in 1964, and currently houses a library.

Plaszow—near Cracow

Plaszow Camp Memorial. Courtesy UJA Archives.

The concentration camp was established in December 1942 on the territory of the Jewish cemetery. It was the last camp established in Poland, and 150,000 persons passed through it in all. Of this number, more than half—or some 80,000—lost their lives before the camp was liquidated in the fall of 1944. (This liquidation was depicted in *Schindler's List*.)

Designed by Ryszard Szczypczynski and Witold Ceckiewicz, a monument now stands on the camp's premises.

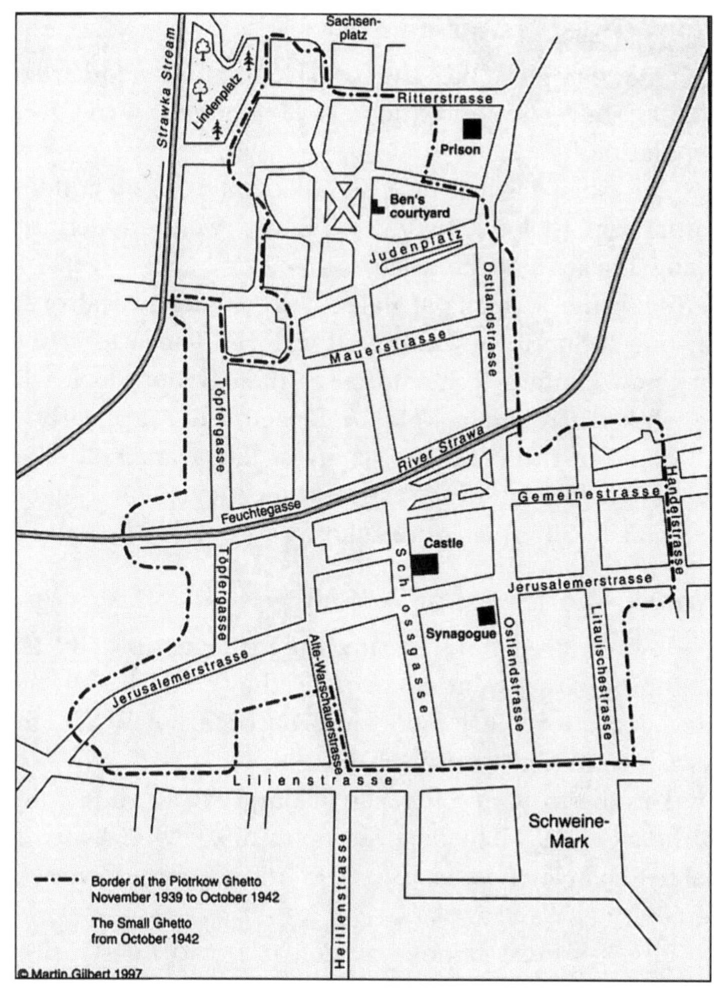

The Piotrkow Ghetto. Courtesy of Martin Gilbert.

Plock—west of Warsaw

On the eve of WWII, the Jewish community comprised 10,000 souls, or approximately 30% of the town's total population.

The old synagogue at J. Kwiatka 7 is a classic building dating back to 1810. Renovated in the twentieth century, it now houses a cooperative.

While the cemetery at Maja 3 was completely destroyed, the one at Sportowa was rebuilt in 1980. The latter cemetery now contains a memorial to the Jews of Plock who perished in Treblinka, Sobibor, Belzec, and Auschwitz.

Some of the famous citizens of Plock are Leib Margulies, the "Mitnaged" to the Hassidic Movement, Shalom Asch, Fish Zilberman, and Yakov Warszawski.

Plonsk—northwest of Warsaw

Jews arrived here in the fifteenth century. By the beginning of the twentieth century, they comprised 64% of the population. Just before the outbreak of WWII, the Jewish community numbered 8,400.

The ghetto was established in May 1940 and liquidated at the end of 1942 by deportation to Auschwitz. A memorial to Shoah victims stands on the grounds of the destroyed cemetery at Warszawska.

Plonsk's most famous citizen is David Ben-Gurion, who was born here in 1886, and went on to become Israel's first prime minister. A monument was erected in his honor as part of the town's celebration of his centennial.

Pniewo

A plaque here marks the mass grave of Jews and some members of the Home Army who were shot between the years 1941 and 1943.

Pokibry

A plaque at the road to Malce commemorates 106 Jewish inhabitants of Cichanowiec who were shot by German gendarmes on December 2, 1942.

Polko (Czorzsztyn County)

A grave here holds the remains of five Jews shot in 1943.

Poloniec

The town's Jewish cemetery contains mass graves.

Poniatowa—west of Mlawa

Originally a Russian POW camp, it became a concentration camp for Jews from Opole Lubelskie at the end of 1942. In April and May 1943, inhabitants of the Warsaw Ghetto were transported here. The Germans shot 18,000 prisoners as they liquidated the camp on September 3, 1943.

Poniatowo

The Trawniki Concentration Camp Memorial stands over a mass grave in the forest outside the village, as well as in the village itself. A third and much larger monument is currently being planned.

Poznan—west of Warsaw

The Jewish community here dates back to 1379.

During the partition of Poland before WWI, Poznan was under German rule. The "Maskilim" Movement was strong (under David Cairo) as a result, and Jewish education was heavily determined by German influences.

On the eve of WWII, there were 1,500 Jews in Poznan. By the end of 1939, the community was entirely destroyed.

The synagogue at Wroniecka was used by the Germans as a swimming pool, and continues to be utilized as such today.

The Jewish cemetery at Glogowska was completely destroyed, and is now part of the Poznan Fairgrounds. Section 5 of the communal cemetery contains a mass grave that contains hundreds of Jews killed during the German occupation.

Pruszca Golanski

Located near the railroad station, a nearby branch of Stutthof contained 300 Jewish women prisoners. A monument there commemorates these victims.

Przasnysz

A memorial at the Jewish cemetery at Leszno bears the inscription, "In memory of those who lived amongst us."

Przemysl—south of Lublin

The first mention of Jews here dates back to the twelfth century. The pre-WWII community was comprised of 20,000 Jews known for their lively political activities, including Folkspartei, Agudat Israel, and Bund.

Under Soviet jurisdiction in 1939–1940, 7,000 Jews were deported to camps and gulags—an action that inadvertently saved some Jewish lives. Those that remained after the Germans attacked the Soviet Union in June 1941 perished in Belzec and Auschwitz.

At Ulica Kopernika 14, a memorial tablet unveiled in 1956 marks the execution place of 2,000 Jews from the ghetto. A monument near Kunkowce honors victims of German executions.

At the main cemetery at Ulica Slowackiego are 200 matzevot, as well as the grave of a Jewish woman and child who were executed along with the three women who hid them. The cemetery also contains twelve mass graves of

Shoah victims. The cemetery at Rakoczego was completely destroyed.

A nineteenth-century synagogue near Wyczolkowski and Maja streets now houses an art gallery.

Przewrotne—north of Rzeszow

A monument honors the partisans of the area, who also enlisted some Jews.

Przyrow—east of Czestochowa

The cemetery at Cmentarna was nearly destroyed.

The Jewish Community Center and house of worship stands at Wlodkowicza 9.

Przysucha—south of Warsaw

The town still holds a synagogue built in 1777.

Pulawy—south of Deblin

Dating back to the nineteenth century, the Jewish community here possessed a number of institutions including schools, a bank, and a trade union. Political parties such as Agudat Israel, Poalei Zion, and Bund were also active. There were 3,600 Jews in town before the war.

Unveiling of monument for the Jews of Pulawy. Courtesy R. Hoenigsfeld-Calandre.

The ghetto was established in October 1939. Its inhabitants were deported to Opole Lubelskie and, at a later stage, to Sobibor.

On the grounds of the destroyed synagogue stands a memorial to local Jews. It was unveiled on August 27, 1987 at the initiative of Mrs. J. Haubenstock.

The cemeteries at Konsko-Wola and Wlostowica were both destroyed.

Pultusk—north of Warsaw

In September 1939, the Germans deported most of the local Jews to the Soviet-occupied Poland. The cemetery was completely destroyed. A memorial to Shoah victims stands at Kotlarska 27.

Punsk

The town's Jewish cemetery has but ten matzevot remaining. The synagogue at Mickiewicza now houses a retail shop.

Pustkow—west of Rzeszow

The death camp was established on November 8, 1940. Before its liquidation on August 23, 1944, approximately 16,000 persons lost their lives there. Unveiled in 1964, a mausoleum honors these Jews, Poles, and Russian POWs.

Pyskowice

At Zadszynz 12, a cemetery contains over 200 graves. Remants of a synagogue built in 1822 still exist.

R

Rabka—southwest of Tarnow

In the forest near Sloneczna, a monument stands at the mass graves of Nazi victims. The former synagogue now serves as private residence.

Rachow-Lipka

A monument honors the local Jews who worked in the nearby mines. The Germans murdered every one of them on October 3, 1943.

Radom—south of Warsaw

The Jewish community dates back to the sixteenth century. Its more celebrated members included Rabbi Shmuel Mohliver and Simha Treistman. The community was served by several institutions including a hospital, a Yeshiva, a few libraries, and a number of newspapers. Before WWII, the town's Jewish population totalled some 30,000 individuals.

The ghetto was established in March 1941. The majority of its inhabitants later perished in Treblinka (28,000) and Auschwitz.

At Bozniczna near Anielewicza, a monument designed by Jacob Zajdensznir stands in honor of the heroes of the Warsaw Ghetto and the 33,000 inhabitants of the Radom Ghetto.

A monument dedicated to Holocaust victims was erected in 1960, and lists the names of the 30,000 Jews of Radom who perished.

Mass graves at the Jewish cemetery at Towarowa mark the spot where 20,000 people were deported during the nights of August 16–17, 1942. Jewish hospital patients and nursing home residents, some 1,000 in all, were killed on the spot.

Radomsko—south of Lodz

Out of the 25,000 citizens of pre-war Radomsko, 9,200 were Jewish. The community enjoyed a rich political life that included Bund and Poalei Zion. It also had a Yeshivah, a Hachsara Kibbutz (in the 1930s), a high school, a private school, and a Hakoach Sports Club.

The Jewish cemetery at Ulica Swierczewskiego was the site of mass executions from 1940 to 1943. During October 1942, a deportation to Treblinka occurred. During the liquidation of the ghetto in January 1943, some 1,500 people were executed.

There were some Jewish partisan units in the area under the command of the Szabatowski brothers.

Radomysl Wielki (Radomishla)—south of Mielec

The community here dates back to the very early part of the seventeenth century, and was an important center of Torah learning. The famous *tzadikim* of Radomysl were Shmuel Engel and Abraham Chaim Horowitz. By 1939, there were some 1,300 Jews in town. Most of them perished in Belzec.

Near the road to Dabrowka Wislocka, the cemetery features a memorial tablet erected in 1987 and approximately 50 remaining matzevot. It also contains the mass graves of Shoah victims who were shot by the Germans in the summer of 1942.

A museum at Ulica Kosciuszki 2 contains a small Judaica exhibition.

Radymno—north of Przemysl

The cemetery was entirely destroyed, though a memorial stone now honors 100 Jews shot there in the fall of 1942.

Radzilow (Rodzilova)—south of Grasewo

The town's Jewish cemetery was completely devastated. A stone marks the mass grave of 800 Jews who were shot and burned alive in a barn in August 1941.

Radzyn Podlaski

A full 50% of the town's population was Jewish when the ghetto was established in the middle of 1940. It was liquidated at the end of 1942 by deportation to Treblinka.

Ratowice

Erected in 1967, a monument here memorializes the victims of Ratowice, where some Polish Jews were imprisoned.

Reszel

The Jewish cemetery at Kosciuszki possesses a couple of matzevot.

Ropczyce (Ropshits)

This town was the seat of Rabbi Naftali Zwi of Robczyce, founder of the Dzikow dynasty.

Ropica Gorna—south of Jasko

An obelisk here marks the grave of three Jews who were shot by German gendarmes in March 1942.

Rutki-Kossaki

The synagogue at Szkolna was reconstructed in the 1960s and is currently utilized as a storage facility.

Rzepiennik Strzyzewski

In the woods of Deby, a mass grave holds the remains of 364 Jews of Gorlice who were murdered on August 11, 1942. The Jewish cemetery near Gromnik-Biecz Road contains 100 matzevot.

Rzeszow—east of Cracow

The Jewish community here dates back to the sixteenth century. By the beginning of the following century, it was a member of the "Council of Four Lands" and was served by a synagogue and other social institutions. The majority of the community was orthodox, though other movements also existed.

The well-known personalities in the town's history were Rabbi Aharon Lewin, who was elected to the Polish Sejm; literary figures, Abba Appelbaum and Itzhak Holzer; and the translator, Moshe Geszwind.

On the eve of WWII, 16,000 Jews called Rzeszow home. The ghetto was established in June 1941. By February 1943, not a single Jew was left, as most had perished in Belzec and Auschwitz.

After the end of the war, 600 Jews returned to Rzeszow; but they emigrated after the anti-Semitic disturbances of June 1945.

There are two synagogues at Plac Zwyciestwa: the seventeenth-century Old Town Synagogue, which presently houses archives; and the New Town Synagogue, which was built in 1710 and presently houses an art gallery.

At the Jewish cemetery at Rejtana, a monument commemorates the Jewish victims of the area. There are approximately 600 matzevot on the grounds.

Mass Graves: see Glogow Malopolski.

Rzymanow

Jews constituted 40% of the town's total population before the outbreak of war. The Germans expelled part of the community to Soviet-occupied Poland. In August 1942, all of the able-bodied men were deported to a labor camp in Plaszow; those remaining were sent to Belzec.

A cemetery at Slowackiego contains some 200 gravestones, as well as monuments that honor Shoah victims and the local Tzadikim.

MAP OF RZESZOW

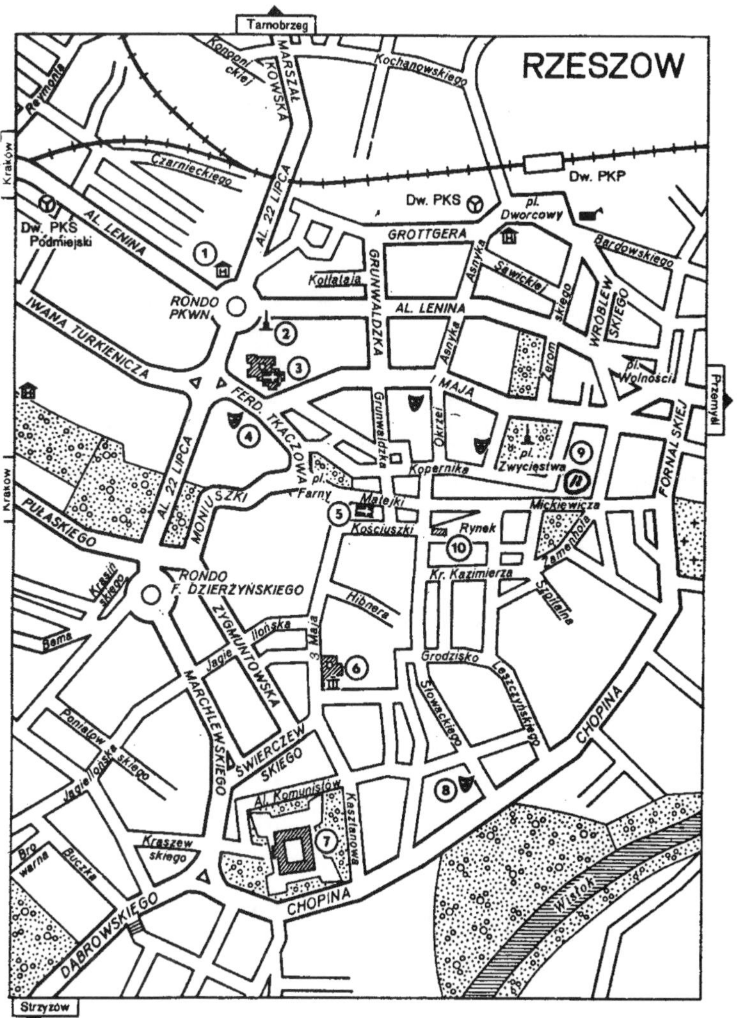

9. *Synagoga Nowomiejska (New Town Synagogue), now an art gallery.*

11. *Synagoga Staromiejska (Old Town Synagogue).*

A ruined synagogue stands at Bieleckigo; on the same street (no. 3) is a small museum that displays a modicum of Jewish memorabilia.

S

Sandomierz (Zuzmir)—southwest of Lublin

Forty Jewish families resided here in 1550. By the end of the 1930s, the Jewish community constituted 34% of the population. Liquidation of the ghetto occurred in January 1943 by deportation to Treblinka.

The synagogue at Basztowa 4 now houses the city's archives. The cemetery at Basztowa was entirely destroyed, while that at Sucha features a few stones and a memorial.

Sanok—southeast of Cracow

By 1570, 18 Jewish families called Sanok home. Before the outbreak of WWII, the Jewish community numbered 50,000 persons. Most of them perished in Belzec.

The former synagogue now serves as a commercial building. The cemetery at Kiczury still contains 50 graves.

Some of the town's famous Jewish citizens include Benjamin Katz, the head of Tel Aviv University, and Rabbi Meir Shapiro.

Sedziszow Malopolski—south of Stalowa Wola

The town's Jewish cemetery stands at Cicha. Inscribed in both Hebrew and Yiddish, a monument at a mass grave honors ghetto victims, including 680 people who were shot on the spot. The remaining inhabitants were deported to Belzec.

Sejny

The cemeteries at Maja 1 and at Zawadzkiego were both destroyed during the war. At Armii Czerwonej, the former synagogue has been converted into a cultural center. The Hebrew High School now serves as a post office.

Sewerynowo (Czerwonka Parish)

At Waski Las, a tablet marks the mass execution of 500 terminally-ill Jews and Poles who were shot in the forest on February 12, 1942.

Siedlce (Shedlitz)—east of Warsaw

The Jewish presence here dates back to the sixteenth century. Before the war, the community numbered some 15,000 persons, or nearly half of the population. It was served by a hospital, Bikur Cholim, Yeshiva, and a pair of Yiddish newspapers. August 1942 witnessed the mass deportation to Treblinka.

In the form of a pyramid of 2,000 Jewish tombstones collected from other destroyed cemeteries, a memorial stands in the local cemetery where 11,000 Jews were shot.

A stone monument at Bohaterow Getta honors 17,000 Jews of Siedlce who were deported to Treblinka. Another monument is located at Berka Joselewicza.

Siemiatycze (Semyatitcha)—south of Bialystok

The Jewish community here was first recorded in the middle of the sixteenth century. Three hundred years later, 75% of the town's citizens were Jews, most of whom dealt in the grain and timber trades.

On the eve of WWII, 7,000 Jews resided here. The ghetto was established in August 1942. It was liquidated in November 1942 by deportation of its inhabitants to Treblinka.

The cemetery at Kosciuszki was almost completely destroyed during the war, though a plaque there commemorates a mass grave of Jews from Siemiatycze. The synagogue at Swierczewskiego was rebuilt after the war.

Sieniawa—south of Lublin

The Jewish cemetery here contains 200 gravestones.

Sieradz—near Lodz

Jews arrived here in the fourteenth century. The Jewish quarter existed by 1812, containing its own cemetery. The community was active in the town's public life, and Israel Kempinski became city counselor in 1862.

There were nearly 3,000 Jews in Sieradz in 1939. The ghetto was liquidated in August 1942.

The synagogue at Ulica Wodna 14 now serves as a cooperative. The cemetery at Ulica Zakladnikow was completely destroyed.

Sieroniowice—north of Gliwice

A symbolic grave here marks the location of a local forced labor camp.

Skala—north of Nowa Huta

At the Jewish cemetery, a mass grave contains the remains of 1,000 victims.

Skarczewy

Near Lake Borowno, a plaque commemorates a few hundred Jews who were executed in October and November 1939. The area was also the site of a slave labor camp.

Skierniewice (Skiernivitz)—north of Lodz

Jews arrived here in the nineteenth century. It was the home of the Hassidic Movement led by Tzadik Shimon Kalisz, who established his court in Skierniewice in 1866.

By 1933, more than 4,000 Jews constituted one-third of the town's total population. The ghetto was established in 1940, and liquidated by deportation of its inmates to the Warsaw Ghetto.

The nineteenth-century synagogue at Batorego 17/19 is currently being restored to house a library.

Skoczow

A modest monument now stands at the former site of the synagogue, which was burned down by the Germans during the 1939 invasion of Poland. It was erected at the initiative of a local resident, Jacek Proszyk.

Slawatycze

The Jewish cemetery here was almost entirely destroyed during the war.

Slubice—west of Warsaw

A mass grave and monument honor vicitims of the German occupation. The cemetery was completely destroyed.

Slupsk—north of Bytow

A monument at Kollataja honors the victims of the local concentration camp, which was a branch of Stutthof. The prisoners there worked on railroad maintenance. Those who survived this back-breaking work lost their lives while being evacuated to Stutthof in April 1945.

The local Jewish cemetery was destroyed.

Slutsk

The town's former synagogue now houses a bakery.

Sobibor Monument, designed by M. Welter.

Sobibor—north of Chelm

The death camp established here in March 1942 existed for eighteen months, during which time some 250,000 Jews were murdered.

A revolt led by the Russian officer Alexander Pieczorski occurred here on October 14, 1943. As a result of this uprising, some 300 prisoners were able to escape.

Sokolow Podloski—east of Wegrow

Jews first immigrated here in the sixteenth century. Before the outbreak of WWII, more than 50% of the population—or 4,000 persons—were Jewish. The mass deportation to Treblinka occurred in September 1942.

Rebuilt after the war, the synagogue at Bohaterow Chodakowa 29 now serves as a store. The nearby cemetery was destroyed, and its grounds are now parkland.

The synagogue at Piekna currently houses stores and apartments. Down the street, a memorial stone honors 1,000 Jews who were killed on September 3, 1942.

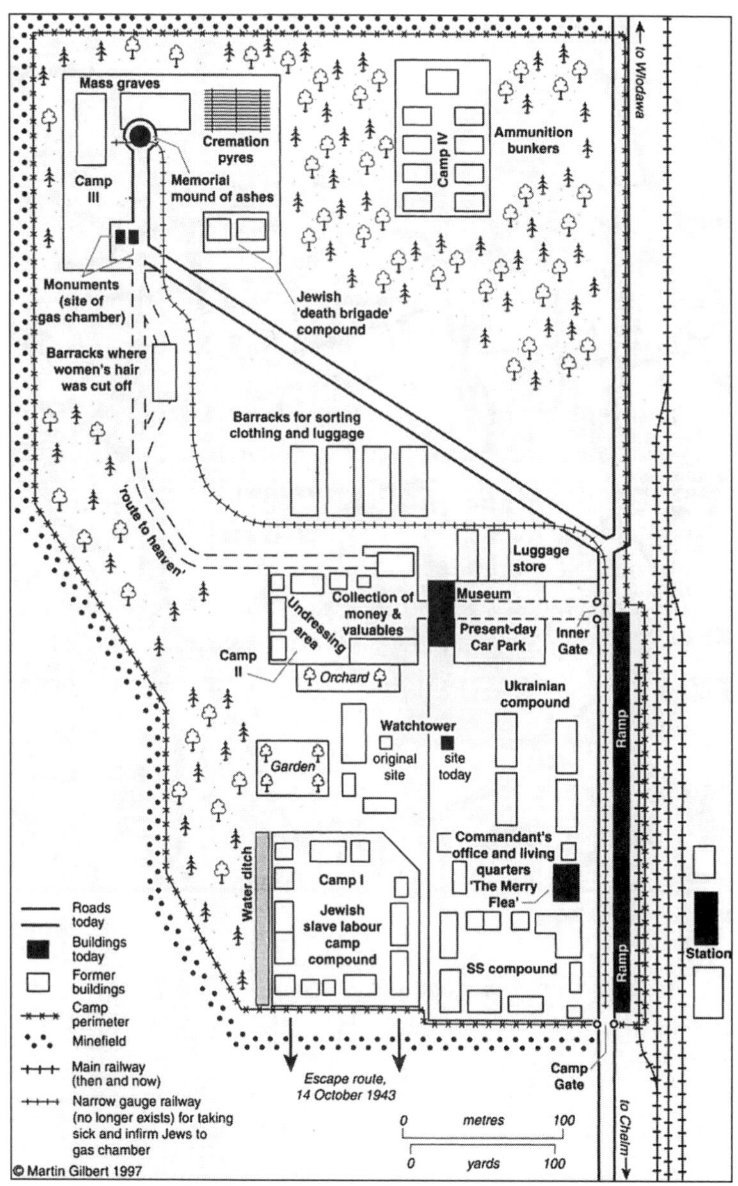

Sobibor. Courtesy of Martin Gilbert.

Sokoly

The cemetery at Nowy Swiat is now utilized as a sports field.

Sosnowiec (Sosnovitz)—near Katowice

By the end of the nineteenth century, nearly 30% of the town's population was Jewish. The community numbered 28,000 persons on the brink of WWII, and was served by schools, an orphanage, a hospital, Yeshivot, and a nursing home.

The bulk of the ghetto's liquidation occurred from August 1–6, 1943, when 10,000 Sosnowiec Jews (of the 24,000 total) were deported to Auschwitz. Only a few survived in bunkers, or under Aryan papers.

An obelisk honors 20,000 local Jews who were murdered.

The surving Jewish cemetery at Gospodarcza contains approximately 300 matzevot. The synagogue, on the other hand, was destroyed in the first days of the German occupation.

Staszow

A holocaust memorial was erected here on the initiative of Jack Goldfarb of B'nai Brith.

Stawice

In the forest near the road to Nowograd, a monument marks the spot of the mass executions of 300 Jews and Poles on July 22, 1943.

Stawiski

A memorial stone here honors 600 Jews who were murdered on August 15, 1941.

The Jewish cemetery at Komzynska still possesses some 50 matzevot. Built in 1879, the local synagogue now serves as a fire station.

Stoczek

The ghetto was liquidated in the fall of 1942, and its inhabitants deported to Treblinka.

At the Jewish cemetery at Wegrowska, a memorial tablet honors these victims.

Strachowice

During the war, some local Jews were forced to work at armament factories. Most perished in Treblinka and Auschwitz.

At Ulica Dr. Anki, a monument to the Freedom Fighters also honors Jews murdered in neighboring labor camps.

The cemetery at Podgorza contains 200 matzevot, while the one at Stycznia 17 possesses approximately 450 gravestones.

Strzyzow—east of Tarnow

The cemeteries at Ulica Wschodnia, Przeclawska, and Daszynskiego were all destroyed during the war. The local synagogue, on the other hand, survived and now serves as a commercial building.

The local museum at Rynek 28 exhibits some Judaica.

Stutthof (Sztutow)—east of Gdansk

Stutthof Concentration Camp was established at the very beginning of the German invasion of Poland. Before the camp was liberated by the Red Army on May 9, 1945, 85,000 people lost their lives there.

A monument designed by Wiktor Tolkin now stands on the spot where the Germans burned the bodies of their victims.

Suwalki—north of Bialystok

At what was Engelsa, a Jewish cemetery exists with only 20 remaining matzevot. The former house of worship now serves as a municipal library.

Swarzedz—east of Poznan

At the local railroad station, a tablet honors the memory of Jews who were forced to work on the railroad tracks from 1941 to 1943. Some of these victims are buried in the back of the Catholic cemetery.

The Jewish cemetery at Poznanska was destroyed, and its grounds are now parkland.

Swidnica

The cemetery at Szarych Szeregow possesses a few dozen matzevot. The house of worship is located at Bohaterow Getta 22.

Szczebrzeszyn

There were approximately 3,000 Jews here, most of whom perished in Belzec.

Established in the sixteenth century, the Jewish cemetery contains several hundred tombstones. The seventeenth-century synagogue now houses a library.

Szczecin (Stetin)—west of Warsaw

The cemetery at Ojca Bejzymy contains a few dozen gravestones. The modern Jewish community and house of worship stands at Niemcewicza 2.

Szczucin—west of Rzeszow

The Jewish community of 800 persons perished in Belzec.

At Maja 1, the Jewish cemetery holds approximately 50 matzevot. There also exists a separate grave that contains the remains of some Polish soldiers and officers who were killed on September 12, 1939, as well as those of the 20 Jews who were forced to bury the other victims.

Szczytno

The cemetery at Lomzynska still possesses a dozen or so matzevot.

Szewnia Gora—west of Zamosc

In the woods near the road from Krasnobor to Zamosc, a monument marks the execution place of Jews, Poles, and Soviet partisans.

Szubin—south of Bydgoszcz

A monument commemorates a so-called "Male (Small) Ghetto," which held approximately 100 local Jews. The Jewish cemetery was completely destroyed during the war.

Szulborze Wielke

Over a mass grave near Mianowka, a monument stands in honor of the Jews of Czyzew, Zareby Koscielne, and Andrzejew, who were killed in the fall of 1941.

Szydlow—near Sandomierz

North of the market square stands a late-Gothic synagogue from the beginning of the sixteenth century. Containing fragments of a late-Renaissance interior, it presently serves as a library.

Szydlowiec—west of Lublin

The ghetto at Wschodnia was liquidated on January 13, 1943, and its inhabitants were deported to Treblinka. Along with a tablet that honors the 16,000 Jews of the

Szydlowiec Ghetto, the Jewish cemetery here contains 2,500 matzevot.

The sixteenth-century synagogue now houses a library.

Szymanowo

At the crossroads of Szymanowo and Sarnowo, a memorial stone marks the place where Jews and Poles were frequently executed.

T

Tarnobrzeg

The Jewish community here numbered 3,800 before the war. The atrocities started on the very first day of the German occupation, when the Wehrmacht executed many Jews in the Town Square.

The synagogue was rebuilt in the 1970s to serve as a library. The cemetery at Sienkiewicza was also destroyed, and its grounds now hold a marketplace.

Tarnograd—southwest of Zamosc

There were 2,500 Jews here before the outbreak of WWII, almost all of whom perished in Treblinka. In addition to these victims, a memorial also honors 82 Jews shot by German gendarmes on September 2, 1942.

The 1686 synagogue now serves as a warehouse. The Jewish cemetery, on the other hand, has survived with approximately 1,000 matzevot.

Tarnow (Tarna)—east of Cracow

The Jewish presence here dates back to the fifteenth century. The community gradually came to possess educational institutions supported by Baron Hirsh, as well as many Zionist organizations—Agudat Hashachar, Ahavat Zion, Bnei Akiva, Bund, Hamizrahi, Hovevei Zion, Hechalutz, and Revisionists, among them.

Before WWII erupted, a full 50% of Tarnow's population was Jewish. The ghetto was liquidated on February 9, 1944, when the remaining 150 Jews were sent to Plaszow. After the war had ended, 700 Jews returned to Tarnow; twenty years later, only 65 remained.

Along with the mass graves of some 15,000 Jews murdered during the German occupation, the old cemetery at Nowodebrowska also contains a memorial that honors all Holocaust victims. A monument at the Jewish cemetery at Szpitalna specifically commemorates the 20,000 slain Jews of Tarnow.

The last remnant of the synagogue—a solitary pillar—still stands and will be permanently preserved through incorporation into a new building to be erected on the site.

At Ulica Goldhamera 5, tablets commemorate both Herman Marz, president of the Jewish community, and Eliasz Goldhamer, its deputy-mayor.

Tarnow contains many other sites of Jewish interest: the old age home stands at Nowodabrowska 25, all of whose occupants were murdered by the Germans; Yavneh High School is located at Ulica Baluta 6; a school and library stands at Ulica Sw. Anny 1; and the former orphanage at Ulica Kollataja 14 presently serves as a kindergarten.

The local museum at the Rynek (City Square) also exhibits some Judaica.

Tomaszow Lubelski—south of Lublin

Jews arrived here in the early seventeenth century, and came to be served by multiple sports clubs and a library. Before the war erupted, the Jewish community embraced 6,000 members.

An obelisk at Kosciuszki honors those executed at the time of the ghetto's liquidation.

Tomaszow Mazawiecki—south of Lodz

At the invitation of Count Antoni Ostrowski, Jews immigrated here in the early seventeenth century. They soon established a textile industry, and eventually boasted a synagogue, a high school, Bet Hamidrash, and some financial institutions.

By 1939, the community consisted of 13,000 people. The ghetto was created in December 1941 and liquidated one year later by deportation to various camps.

The Germans immediately burned the town's synagogue, though some Sifrei Torah were saved and recovered after the war.

Established in 1831 on grounds donated by Count Ostrowski, the cemetery at Smutna 19 is walled off and features 2,000 matzevot.

Torun—south of Gdansk

Approximately 1,000 Jews called Torun home on the eve of WWII, at which time the community was served by a synagogue, an educational system, and other social institutions.

The local Jewish cemetery was completely destroyed. A mass grave here holds the remains of 152 Jewish women from Charobio who were killed before the evacuation of the work camp on January 18, 1945.

Trawniki—west of Chelm

Trawniki was the site of a concentration camp that was originally created for Soviet POWs in June 1941. In the fall of 1942, it was converted into a work camp for Jews from Poland, Austria, Germany, Czechoslovakia, Belgium, Holland, and France. Those prisoners who remained—10,000 in all—were murdered on November 3, 1943. A monument now marks the site of this mass execution. (See Poniatowo.)

Treblinka

Treblinka I was a forced labor camp created in 1941. Before its liquidation in July 1944, some 20,000 victims passed through its gates.

Treblinka II was a death camp established in the spring of 1942. The Nazis built an imaginary railroad station and camouflaged it as a small rural station. Timetables and

Symbolic graves for the lost communities at Treblinka.

advertisements were posted on its walls to disguise its real purpose. From across the European continent, freight trains deposited victims here. The camp operated thirteen gas chambers.

An armed revolt occurred on August 2, 1943, during which some prisoners managed to escape. Before the camp was liberated a few weeks later, 876,600 persons—most of them from Warsaw— perished there.

On the site of the former center of immediate extermination here, stands a symbolic cemetery for the approximately 750,000 to 900,000 murdered Jews from Poland, Germany, Austria, Czechoslovakia, France, the Netherlands, Belgium, the former USSR, and Yugoslavia.

A nearby monument consists of 17,000 stones marked with the cities and countries from which Jews originated. A map at the entrance to the camp shows the specific location of the stones, one of which is devoted to Janusz Korczak and his children. The central part of the monument takes form of a menorah inscribed "Never Again" in a host of languages, including Yiddish.

Trzebinia (Chebin)—west of Cracow

Opposite the refinery at Kruczkowskiego, an obelisk honors Jewish victims of the labor camp, which existed from 1942 to 1945.

The cemetery at Slowackiego possesses 200 matzevot in various stages of decay.

Turek—south of Torun

A monument at Kolska commemorates execution victims who fell in the market place between 1939 and 1940.

While the cemetery lies destroyed, the synagogue serves as a cooperative.

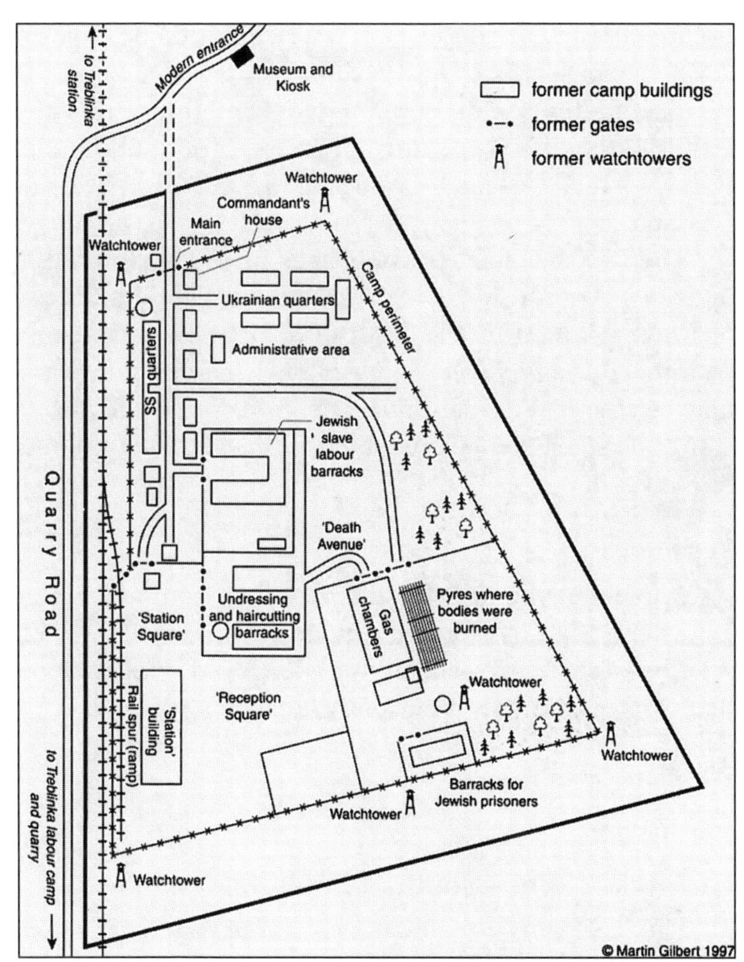

Treblinka. Courtesy of Martin Gilbert.

Tykocin (Tiktin)—near Bialystok

The Jewish community here was established in 1552, and came to be served by a "Tarbut" school and a Zionist organization. On the eve of WWII, it numbered some 2,500 persons.

The memorial at Lopuchowo commemorates the 1,600 Jews who were murdered by "Kommando Bialystok," which was led by Wolfgang Birkner of the Warsaw Gestapo.

The Jewish cemetery established in 1522 features 500 matzevot. Built at Kozia in 1642, an early Baroque house of prayer stands in the form of a fortress. Beautifully restored, it is a typical example of Jewish architecture and now serves as a Jewish museum. Well worth the trip, a stop at Tykocin can be combined with a visit to Treblinka or Bialystok.

Tyszowce

A tablet at the parish building offices commemorates 1,000 Jews shot by German gendarmes on June 16, 1942.

The local Jewish cemetery was destroyed; at least a portion of its old grounds is currently home to a pre-school.

U

Ustrzyeki-Dolne—south of Przemysl

The local synagogue now houses a library. The Jewish cemetery still possesses approximately 80 gravestones.

Uzarzewo

A tablet at a mass grave commemorates Jews murdered in the labor camps of Groszczyna and Kobylnica.

W

Walbrzych—south of Lublin

The local community and house of worship stands at Mickiewicza 18.

Warka (Vorki)

Rabbi Itzhak, better known as the Silent Tzaddik, resided here before his death in 1848.

Warsaw (Warszawa)

See Chapter Five, page 163.

Warta—west of Zdunska Wola

The Jewish community here dates back to the thirteenth century, and erected its first synagogue in 1534. Warta's Jews enjoyed a rich political life that included the Bund and Zionist Movements. They were also active in the independence movement of the nineteenth century, for which a few suffered deportation to Siberia.

There were 2,000 Jews in the town on the eve of WWII. In May 1942, the Germans executed a number of these inhabitants, including the heroic Rabbi Laskowski. The community's remnants perished in Chelmno.

The cemetery at Ulica Gorna 7 was entirely destroyed during the war; while that at Ulica Sadowa still features 170 matzevot.

The synagogue now serves as a private residence.

Wasosz

The town contains a mass grave of 250 Jews who were shot by the Wehrmacht in August 1941.

Wesola—north of Tarnow

A monument here honors local Jews who were shot in the fields in August 1942.

Wieliczka—south of Nowa Huta

Together with some 7,000 other Jews from the region, the 1,300 Jews of Wieliczka were deported almost exclusively to Belzec. The remaining minority was sent to labor camps in Plaszow and Stalowa Wola.

Wielki Gleboczek (Brzozie Parish)

On the wall of a school located on the former grounds of the labor camp, a memorial tablet honors Jewish women who perished there. The camp was liquidated in January 1945.

Wielkie Oczy—south of Tomaszow Lubelski

The cemetery here possesses a few matzevot, as well as a tablet for 41 Jews shot by German gendarmes. The synagogue now serves as a silo.

Wielun—south of Sieradz

The Jewish community was established in the sixteenth century, and consisted of 4,200 people before the outbreak of war. Most of them perished in Chelmno.

An obelisk honors Shoah victims. At Ulica Kijok 17, the Jewish cemetery was completely destroyed.

Wieruszow—south of Kalisz

Before the war erupted, there were 3,000 Jews here—most of whom were eventually murdered in Chelmno.

Along with 200 matzevot, the Jewish cemetery contains a commemorative plaque that honors victims of the town's ghetto.

Wiewiorka—south of Mielec

An obelisk here honors 18 people who were murdered on March 23, 1943, after the Germans accused them of assisting partisans and hiding Jews.

Wiszenski

A tablet marks the execution spot of 30 persons accused of helping Jews and Soviet POWs.

Wlodawa—northeast of Lublin

On the eve of WWII, the Jewish community here numbered nearly 6,000—most of whom eventually perished in Sobibor. A Jewish partisan unit was active in the area under the command of Yehiel Grynszpan.

For nearly 50 years, the local synagogue stood in ruins. Recently rebuilt through private contributions, the building now houses a regional museum. It features a permanent exhibition of Judaica, which is comprised of articles donated from Wlodawa's Jewish residents.

Wodzislaw—southwest of Kielce

At the Jewish cemetery, there is a grave for victims of the German executions that occurred here in September and October 1943.

The sixteenth-century synagogue has been abandoned.

Wolbrom

The Jewish community here consisted of 5,000 people. The ghetto existed from 1941 until September 1942, when the Germans murdered 2,000 people. The remainder of those imprisoned were deported to Belzec.

The Jewish cemetery contains a mass grave for victims of the area.

Wroclaw (Breslau)—south of Poznan

The Jewish community here dates back to the twelfth century. A German city in the 1930s, it was exposed to the earliest of Nazi atrocities. During *Kristalnacht*, Nazis burned and demolished Jewish houses of prayer and living quarters. In 1941, the community was deported to the Riga Ghetto and Terezin.

When the territory was ceded to Poland at the end of the war, a sizable Jewish community reemerged with the repatriation of Jews from the Soviet Union. It was subsequently depleted, however, by waves of emigration in the 1950s and in 1968.

The modern Jewish community of Wroclaw consists of approximately 1,000 people—large by today's Polish standards. Of this number, about 100 are young.

Built in 1827 by architect Karol Gotthard, a Jewish Community Center and neo-classical synagogue still stand at Wlodkowicza 9. Also present here is a kosher kitchen that serves approximately 60 meals per day.

Built in 1726 at Ulica Wisniowa, the Jewish Hospital (Israelitsches Krankenhaus) now serves as a railroad hospital.

The cemetery at Ulica Lotnicza 51 still possesses some 8,000 graves. A Jewish cemetery at Slezna and Sztabowa Streets contains some great examples of nineteenth-century gravestone art. Many famous members of the Wroclaw community are buried here: Heinrick Graetz, a renowned historian; Ferdinand Lassale, a leader of the German Labor Movement and a participant in the "Spring of Nations"; Jan Gotfryd Gallea, discoverer of the planet Neptune; and Max Moszkowski, explorer of Sumatra.

At Plac Grunwaldzki, a memorial commemorates those murdered in Lvov (Lwow) in the summer of 1941—all Polish scientists and men of letters, including some Jews—with earth from the execution place.

A Warsaw Ghetto monument stands near Plac Bohaterow Getta, which was named in honor of the ghetto heroes.

Wroclawek

The communal cemetery holds 24 individual and three mass graves, one of which contains the remains of Jews from the Rakutowek Ghetto.

Wrzesnia—south of Gniezno

At the western end of the railroad station, a gravestone honors victims of a labor camp for Jews known as the "Julag."

Wysokie Mazowieckie

The Jewish cemetery at Zwirki i Wigury contains approximately 20 matzevot.

Wyszkow

This town is the home of 5,000 Holocaust victims, as well as that of Mordechai Anielewicz, the leader of the Warsaw Ghetto Uprising.

Established in the nineteenth century, the cemetery at Lakowa was almost completely destroyed during the war. Under the auspices of the United States Commission for the Preservation of America's Heritage Abroad, the cemetery has been painstakingly restored.

Z

Zablotczyzna

The town contains a mass grave of 500 Jews who were murdered on August 5, 1941.

Zabludow

On the eve of WWII, 2,000 Jews resided here. Most of them were deported to Treblinka on November 2, 1942.

A Jewish cemetery on the western outskirts of town survived the war and holds fifty remaining matzevot.

Zabno

In addition to a cemetery, the town is home to a mass grave of approximately 100 Jews who were murdered by the Nazis on March 11–12, 1942.

Zagorow—southwest of Konin

At Plac Maciejewskiego, a monument honors freedom fighters, as well as 2,500 Jews from the ghetto who were shot in October 1941.

Zagorz—south of Sanok

At the mass grave at Ulica Fabryczna, a memorial marks the spot where 4,000 Holocaust victims were executed between 1940 and 1944.

Zamosc—south of Lublin

After a "privilege" was granted in 1588, the Jewish community grew quickly here to include a synagogue and other social organizations. The eighteenth and nineteenth centuries witnessed the introduction of Sephardic Jews into the city, as well as a multitude of political and religious movements. On the eve of WWII, approximately 60% of the city's total population was Jewish.

Built in the early seventeenth-century in the Post-Renaissance style, a later synagogue was destroyed during the German occupation. It was rebuilt between 1950 and 1965 in its original form, which included stucco-work and murals. Standing in a neighborhood with streets named after Dr. Zamenhof and Perec, the building now houses a library.

The Museum of Martyrology stands at the "Rotunda," the location of mass executions of Poles, Jews, and POWs.

A monument honors prisoners of the transit camp, which was used by the Germans during the deportation from Zamosc. Another monument commemorates the city's 10,000 Jews who were murdered in the ghetto and in Belzec.

A monument at Ulica Szwedska honors Russian POWs who were interned at the local camp in 1943. (The Wehrmacht immediately shot officers and Jewish POWs upon arrival.) In the woods of Rapy, a monument marks the execution place of Jews and partisans in 1944.

A plaque at an agricultural school, which was utilized as an SS riding camp, commemorates Jews and POWs who were forced to work there.

A plaque at the Stara Brama Lubelska memorializes hundreds of Poles, Jews, and Russian POWs who were shot on the premises of Zamoyskiego High School by German gendarmes.

Some famous personalities identified with Zamosc are Rabbi Zvi Hirsh, Rabbi Yacov Krantz (known as "Hamagid from Dubna"), Rabbi Isaac Zamosc, and the famous literary figure, Icchak Leib Perec.

Zarki—south of Czestochowa

Though there were only 600 Jews here before the war, the community had a high school and library that featured a collection of six thousand books. Both of these institutions were founded by Abraham Joseph Sztybel.

The cemetery at Ulica Polna contains 900 matzevot, and was cleaned and renovated through the efforts of Eli Zborowski of New York. The nineteenth-century synagogue underwent renovation in 1950 and now serves as a cultural house.

Zary

A Jewish Community Center and house of worship currently stand at Armii Czerwonej 3A.

Zarzecze—south of Zamosc

A monument here honors the inmates of a labor camp for Czech and Austrian Jews.

Zaslow

The Martyrs Memorial here honors 10,000 Jews, Poles, and Gypsies who were murdered by the Nazis in nearby Sanok.

Zawiercie

In 1921, some 21% of the town's population was Jewish. The ghetto was created in the summer of 1940, and held both Polish and Czech Jews. Shortly thereafter, 500 inmates were sent to slave labor camps in Germany. In May 1942, approximately 2,000 people were deported to Auschwitz. The ghetto was officially liquidated in August 1943.

Built in 1880, the synagogue at Duracza now serves as an office building. Near the synagogue stands a Jewish Community Center.

The cemetery at Dzierzynskiego 56 possesses approximately 200 matzevot, while that at Piaskowa 32 contains nearly 1,000.

Zbylitowska Gora

In the woods of Buczyna, a mausoleum marks the mass grave and place of executions in the years 1942–1944. In all, it honors some 10,000 people, including 800 Jewish children who were murdered there.

Zdroj

An obelisk here commemorates 1,400 Jews who were shot on August 10, 1942.

Zdunska Wola—east of Sieradz

The Jewish presence here began only in the nineteenth century. By 1939, however, it had grown to encompass 10,000 people, or 40% of the town's population. The community was served by Hebrew schools, a banking cooperative, and a synagogue.

Built in 1858 near the railroad station, the synagogue now houses a storage facility. Established in the same year, the cemetery at Ulica Kacza now features approximately 400 graves.

Zgierz—north of Lodz

At the intersection of Barona and Plaskowa stands a surviving Jewish cemetery.

Zolkiewka—west of Zamosc

A monument here honors Jews from the local ghetto.

Zwiernik—north of Jaslo

The town possesses a grave of three Jews and the Pole who hid them—all of whom were shot by the Germans in 1943.

Zwolen—west of Pulawy

The Jewish community here dates back to 1554. On the eve of WWII, it comprised 3,800 persons, or 51% of the population. Most of them perished in the labor camps at Pustkowie and Treblinka.

CHAPTER 5

Major Jewish Centers

CRACOW (KRAKOW/KROKE)

The Jewish community here dates back to the eleventh century, and reached the peak of its development in the sixteenth century. With the transfer of Poland's capital to Warsaw in 1596, Cracow declined somewhat. Nonetheless, the city contained a Hebrew high school, a commercial school (with 2,000 students), a Mizrahi school, Yeshiva, a Jewish theater, a Jewish hospital and library, and two Jewish newspapers—*Woche* and *Nowy Dziennik*.

In addition to these institutions, the Jews of Cracow were active in political groups such as Bund, B'nai Brith, Poalei Zion, Mizrahi, as well as Zionist organizations: Beitar, Menora, Brith Hayal, and Vered, among them.

Some important Jewish citizens of Cracow were Lewko, who administered the Royal Mint for Casimir the Great; merchants, Pinkas Horowic and Isaac Jakubowicz; Hebrew printers and sons of Chaim of Halicz: Asher, Eliakim, and Samuel; Menachem Meisels; and Izaak Prostitz. Another Jewish protege of a Polish king was Michael Ezofowica, who was knighted by King Sigismund I in 1525.

On the eve of WWII, 56,000 of the 300,000 inhabitants of Cracow were Jewish. One restricting decree followed another, until the Cracow Ghetto was established in March 1941 in the Podgorze area. Mass deportation to Belzec occurred in the first week of June 1942.

Most of the Jewish points of interest are located in Kazimierz, once a separate Jewish town within Cracow. Kazimierz was established by Casimir III the Great's charter of 1335. The king's benevolence towards the Jews was supposedly based on his love for the Jewish Esther, who, according to the same legend, lived at Ulica Krakowska 46.

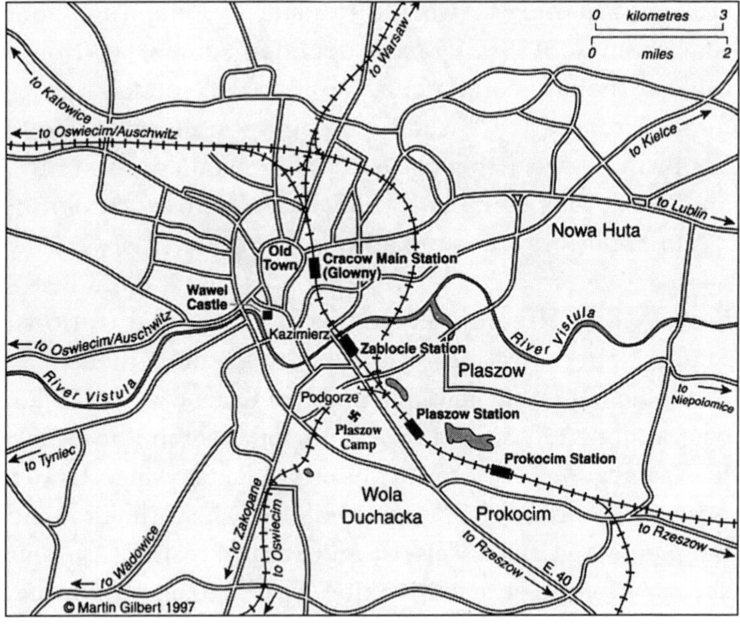

The Cracow Region. Courtesy of Martin Gilbert.

CEMETERIES

New Jewish Cemetery

Established in 1800, the cemetery at Miodowa 55 still serves as a Jewish burial place. The oldest matzevot here date back to the nineteenth century.

Some of Cracow's most famous citizens are buried here: Dr. Nussenfield, director of the Jewish hospital; Maurycy Gottlieb, one of the best Jewish painters in the world, and a student of Poland's national painter, Jan Matejko; Rabbi Ozjasz Thon, the spiritual leader of the progressive movement in Cracow and a member of the Polish Sejm (parliament); and Maciej Jakobowicz, one-time president of Poland's Jewish community.

The cemetery, which was devastated during the occupation, was restored thanks to the assistance of the American Joint Distribution Committee. A memorial to Shoah victims stands near the entrance.

Old Jewish Cemetery (Kirkut Remuh)

Adjoining the Remuh Synagogue at Szeroka 40, this cemetery dates back to 1533, making it the oldest existing Jewish burial ground in Poland. The grounds were in use between 1552 and 1800.

Part of the cemetery now is a wall built from pieces of the gravestones that were destroyed by the Nazis. In fact, the only tombstone that has survived virtually unscathed is that of Rabbi Moses Isserless (1510–1572), who is particularly remembered for his commentary on the supplement to Joseph Caro's *Shulhan Arukh*. Rabbi Isserless' epitaph reads: "From Moses to Moses, there was none like Moses."

Old Cemetery by the Remuh Synagogue in Cracow.

A number of other leaders of the Cracow Jewish community are also buried here:

- **Deiches, Mordechai**: son of Naphtali, and rabbi of Cracow in the seventeenth century.
- **Enzels, Mozes**: son of Naphtali, rabbi of Cracow from 1694–1706.
- **Halevy (Halewi), Izaak**: son of Mordechai, rabbi of Cracow and head of the Yeshiva from 1766 to 1799.
- **Heller, Gershon Saul Yom Tov Lipman** (1579–1654): son of Nathan, he was a leader of communities in Vienna and Prague. He also served as rabbi of

Cracow from 1643–1654, for most of which time he also headed the Yeshiva.

➢ **Landau, Izaak**: son of Zvi Hirsh, rabbi of Cracow from 1754–1768.

➢ **Saba, Mordechai**: known as Singer, head of the Yeshiva from 1572 to 1576.

➢ **Sirkes, Joel (1561–1640)**: known as Bach, rabbi of the Jewish community from 1618 to 1640. He was also an authority on Talmudic law.

➢ **Spiro, Natan Nate (1591–1633)**: son of Rabbi Solomon, head of the Yeshiva from 1617 to 1633.

Note: A destroyed Jewish cemetery is located at Ulica Jerozolimska.

GHETTO

The Cracow Ghetto was established on March 13, 1943. Few survived of the 68,000 Jews interned here; most were murdered in the camps of Belzec, Sobibor, Majdanek, Auschwitz-Birkenau, and nearby Plaszow.

The Jewish Combat Organization (Z.O.B.)—under the leadership of Dolek Liebeskind, Shimson Dranger, Heshek Bauminger, and Benek Halbreich—operated in the area, trying to organize resistance and eliminate informers. A commemorative tablet in honor of these ghetto heroes has been placed on their headquarters.

Among the local Jews who were murdered was the great Yiddish poet, Mordechai Gebirtig, whose song “S’ Brennt” (“It Burns”) became the anthem of Jewish resistance:

Andante
Es brent bri - der es brent.
brent bri - der es brent.
S'ken cho - li - le ku - men der mo - ment.
Dos iz nor in aich a - lein ge - vendt.
Ven dos shte - tl mit aich tzu - za - men
Ven dos shte - tl iz aich ta - ier
zol a - vek mit ash un fla - men
nemt die kei - lim lesht dos fa - ier,
Blai-bn zol a pus-ter shliad shvar-tze pus-te vent.
Lesht mit ai - er ei - gn blut ba vaist vos ihr kent.
Un ihr shteit un kukt a - zoi zich mit far-leig-te
Shteit nit bri - der ot a - zoi zich mit far-leig-te
hent. Un ihr shteit un kukt a-zoi zich vie
hent. Shteit nit bri-der un kukt a-zoi zich vie
un - zer shte - tl brent.
un - zer shte - tl brent.
Es

It Burns

It burns, brothers, it burns.
The time of anguish—God Forbid—now churns
When the village and you in one blow
Turn to ashes, to flames all aglow.
Nothing will remain at all—
Just a blackened wall—

And you look and you stand,
Each with folded hand.
And you look and you stand,
At burned village and land.
It burns, brothers, it burns,
To you alone this agony turns.
If you love your town, its name,
Take the vessels, quench the flame.
Quench it with your own blood too:

Show what you can do.
Brothers, do not look and stand,
Each with folded hand.
Brothers, do not look and stand
While the town burns and the land.

MEMORIALS

Café Cyganeria

Across the street from the municipal theater, a tablet here reads: "On the night between the 24th and 25th of December 1942, a group of soldiers from the People's Army and the Jewish Fighting Organization carried out an operation on the Cynageria Hall, which was full of Germans, and inflicted heavy losses upon the conqueror."

All those who participated in this mission were Jews, led by Adolf Liebeskind and Jehuda Lieber.

The Heroes of the Ghetto Square

Plac Bohaterow Getta 6 marks the spot from which the Jews of Cracow were deported to Auschwitz and Belzec.

Mickiewicz Monument

The city's main square (Rynek Glowny) commemorates Adam Mickiewicz, Poland's national poet, who was one of the great champions of Jewish rights in the country's history. His national epic, *Pan Tadeusz*, has been translated into many languages, including English and Hebrew.

Plaszow

See glossary entry, page 92.

Podgorze

Located at Ulica Lwowska 25/29, a plaque is affixed to the remains of a wall of the Cracow Ghetto, which existed from March 3, 1941 to March 14, 1943. The remaining ghetto inhabitants were killed on the spot, or sent to death camps in Belzec, Majdanek, and Sobibor.

MUSEUMS

Headquarters of the Jewish Combat Organization

Located near the pharmacy at Bohaterow Getta 6, a commemorative plaque was affixed to the wall on the fifth anniversary of the ghetto's liquidation. It also houses a modest museum with a plaque that states that the Jewish Fighting Organization was founded here.

One of the leading figures of the Z.O.B. in Cracow was Bernard Halbreich, an N.C.O. in the Polish army who was killed in action in February 1943.

The Judaica Branch of the Historical Museum of Cracow

The museum is housed in the Old Synagogue at 24 Szeroka in the Kazimierz section of Cracow. The synagogue was originally erected in the fifteenth century, and was modeled on older synagogues in Worms, Regensburg, and Prague. After a fire, it was rebuilt by Matteo Gucci of Florence. During World War II, the synagogue was partially destroyed and profaned by the Germans; its courtyard served as an execution place. The building was renovated in 1956, mainly due to the efforts of Boleslaw Drobner, a Jewish Seym deputy.

The permanent exhibition covers the pre-war history of Kazimierz, as well as the fate of Cracow Jews in Plaszow and other death camps. In addition, the museum contains a collection of Judaica from the seventeenth, eighteenth, and twentieth centuries. Among these items are works of master jewelers who specialized in Judaica, including Kelmer, Lopienski, Pogorzelski, Reidel, Szekman, and Szyldberg.

Display in the Jewish Museum Cracow, Old Synagogue.

A plaque here commemorates the visit of Tadeusz

Kosciuszko Plaque at the Old Synagogue in Cracow.

Kosciuszko, hero of the Polish Uprising (and of the American Revolution), who came to call the Jewish population to arms in 1794. The plaque reads: "The Jews proved to the world that whenever humanity could gain, they would not spare their lives. Here, in the old synagogue, in the days of the insurrection of 1794, Tadeusz Kosciuszko called the Jews to arms in the fight for the liberation of the country."

SECULAR BUILDINGS

Ariel Café

This "Israeli-style" gathering place stands at Szeroka 17.

Grodzka 62

Before the war, this building housed the Jewish printing press owned by the Jozef Fiszer family. It printed many famous works, including those of Ahad Haam, Bialik, Mendel Mocher Sefarim, and Shalom Aleichem.

High School

Located at the cross section of Brzozowa and Podbrzezie, this site was the center of Jewish education. The Hebrew gymnasium stood at Podbrzezie 8/10; the crafts high school at No. 3; the primary school at Brzozowa 5; and the "Mizrahi" school at Ulica Miodowa 26. Solomon Deiches Beth Hamdrash was also located in this area.

The Jewish Community Building

Before the outbreak of WWII, this site at Skawinska 2 housed a Jewish library. It now serves as a kosher kitchen with the assistance of the American Joint Distribution Committee.

Jewish Hospital

At Skawinska 8, stood a Jewish hospital named Israelite Hospital, which was built in 1822. After WWII, its remaining archives were transferred to the Jewish Historical Institute in Warsaw. The building currently houses the Municipal Medical Department.

Jewish Social and Cultural Association

Located at Dluga 38, this site has been restored under the auspices of the Ronald Lauder Foundation.

Jewish Theater

The theater, at Bochenska 7, has witnessed such Jewish theatrical talents as Djigan, Ida Kaminsky, Shumacher, and the Turkows.

Pankiewicz Pharmacy

Located at Bohaterow Getta 18, this "Pharmacy under the Eagle," stood on the border of the Cracow Ghetto.

Ritual Slaughter House

Located at Plac Nowy 11, this site now serves as a market hall.

Ronald S. Lauder Foundation Community Youth Center

The center stands at Kupa 18. For more information, see "Polish Jewry Today," page 20.

State's Children Home #2

A memorial plaque honors Janusz Korczak at Chmielewskiego 6.

Student's House

Before the eruption of WWII, the building at Ulica Przemyska 2 provided housing for 140 Jewish students at Jagiellonian University. It now houses students of the School of Music.

STREETS

Berka Joselewicza

This street was named in honor of Colonel Berek Joselewicz, who commanded a Jewish regiment in Kosciuszko's Revolt against the Russians in 1794.

Izaka

This thoroughfare is named after Rabbi Isaac of Prossnitz, who founded Poland's first Jewish printing shop in 1530.

Joselewicza

This street also honors the Jewish colonel—a hero of the Kosciuszko Uprising.

Stet Meiselsa

Dov Berush Meisels, a rabbi of the mid-nineteenth century, gives his name to this street. He served in the senate of the Republic of Cracow, and was one of the leaders of the Polish liberation movement.

Szpitalna

Before the eruption of WWII, this street contained many Jewish-owned shops that specialized in secondhand books.

Zamenhofa

Doctor Ludwik Zamenhof, the father of Esperanto, lends his name to this thoroughfare.

SYNAGOGUES

Boznica Kupa

Located at Jonatana Warszauera 8, it was built from community funds—the "kupa"—in 1647. Before the war, the building was used by "Mizrahi"; today, it houses a cooperative.

Boznica Wysoka

A high synagogue built from 1556 to 1563, the building at Jozefa 38 now serves as a reconstruction workshop for works of art.

Chevrah Tehilim

The former synagogue at Mieselsa 18 now houses a dance group.

Isaak's Synagogue

Located at Jakuba 25, it was built from 1638 to 1644 under the auspices of Izaak Jakubowicz, banker to King Wladyslaw IV. The design is that of Francesco Olivieri.

Renovated somewhat after the war, it now serves as a sculptor's studio; though a more thorough reconstruction is underway for possible use as a library.

Poper's Synagogue

Merchant Wolf (Bocian) Poper constructed the building at Szeroka 16 in 1620. Renovated after the war—only "Aron Hakodesh" has survived among the original fixtures—it now serves as a youth house.

Remuh Synagogue

Located at Szeroka 40, it was built in 1557 by Rabbi Isserless' father, a banker to King Sigismund II Augustus. The name is a contraction of Rabbi Moses Isserless, who preached and taught here—"Rama" as he is shown in *The Early Achronim*.

It was restored in 1870 by Mateusz Crucci, and still serves as a house of worship.

Sheerit Bnei Emuna

This nineteenth-century synagogue, at 17 Rabbi Meisels Street, has served as the headquarters of the Judaica Foundation Center for Jewish Culture since 1993. The Center's goals are civic-minded initiatives: to preserve the still-existing Jewish heritage in Kazimierz; to disseminate knowledge about Jewish history and culture among the younger generations; to protect the memory of the centuries-old Jewish presence in Poland; to serve as a platform for Polish-Jewish dialogue; and to fight any form of anti-Semitism, discrimination, and intolerance. In order to achieve these goals, the Center offers extensive educational and cultural programs that encompass lectures, conferences, book presentations, summer programs for foreign students, concerts, film screenings, and many

Remuh Synagogue in Cracow.

other special events. A corollary association has recently been established in the United States to help support the Foundation: the American Friends of the Judaica Foundation on Cracow.

Stained-Glass Window in the Tempel Synagogue in Cracow.

The Tempel

Located at Miodowa 24, it is usually open on major holidays, when the tiny Remu Synagogue cannot hold the worshippers. It was originally constructed in 1862 as a progressive (*Postepowa*) synagogue, but is now orthodox.

Near the temple, a modern mikvah was constructed. (The pre-war mikvah was located at Szeroka 6). The Meiselsa Center was also added to the Jewish Center here.

OTHER POINTS OF INTEREST

Sites from *Schindler's List*

The Oscar-winning movie, *Schindler's List*, was filmed in Kazimierz and Cracow. The film's list of sights:

- The building of the former "Deutsche Emalienwaren Fabrik" at Lipowa-Szeroka
- The former concentration camp in Plaszow

- ➢ The ghetto area in the Podgorze district
- ➢ "Liban" quarry
- ➢ Schindler's house at Straszewskiego 7
- ➢ Szeroka Street
- ➢ Wolnica Square
- ➢ Yard at Meiselsa Street

Festival of Jewish Culture

Begun in 1990, the Jewish Cultural Festival in Cracow is the only comprehensive Jewish festival in Central and Eastern Europe. As such, it draws tens of thousands of visitors from throughout the world. These celebrants are treated to both traditional and contemporary works of synagogue music, klezmer music, folk music, chamber music, and jazz—as well as drama, film, dance, and literature.

For further information on the festival contact the Jewish Cultural Festival Society at 31-107 Cracow / ul. Sw. Getrudy 5; at mak@smok.krakus.top.pl; or by tel/fax at (48-12) 429-2573.

LODZ

Jews immigrated to Lodz relatively late, and there were only 11 Jews here as late as 1793. The reason for the community's minimal presence was that the Kujawy bishops owned the rural village and the subsequent town. In the nineteenth century, however, the Jewish community began to develop in earnest. Its main occupations were crafts and industry.

With this increased coherence and strength, Jews made a considerable mark on the spiritual and material face of Lodz. The careers of many powerful Jewish industrialists began here, including Poznanski, Kohn, Kentenberg, Silberstein, Jarocinski, Prussak, and Landau.

On the eve of WWII, Lodz was home to the second largest Jewish community in Poland—250,000 individuals out of a total population of 670,000. The second ghetto to be established in Poland, the Lodz Ghetto eventually held Lodz Jews, as well as 20,000 Jews from Germany, Austria, Czechoslovakia, Holland, and Luxembourg. It was the very last ghetto to be liquidated in August 1944. During its long existence, the ghetto was ruthlessly ruled by M.C. Chaim Rumkowski, "the eldest of the Jews," whose signature even appeared on its currency.

When Lodz was liberated on January 19, 1945, only 800 Jews remained.

CEMETERIES

Jewish cemeteries are practically the only material evidence of the Jewish past in Lodz. They are rich with monuments that contain a great number of individual signs, religious inscriptions, and historical messages.

New Jewish Cemetery

Located at Bracka and Zmienna, it encompasses 101 acres or, together with the building on the grounds, 105.6 acres.

During World War I, the wooden fence surrounding the cemetery was destroyed. Short on finances, the community subsequently protected it with an inadequate earthen wall. Only in 1922 could adequate funds be raised to erect a brick wall that, along with 15 to 20 attendants, maintained the cemetery until WWII.

During the Nazi occupation, the cemetery was within the boundaries of the ghetto. As starvation and disease

Cemetery Gate at Lodz.

decimated the ghetto's population in those tragic days, the plots along Bracka filled up quickly. Between 1940 and 1943, 40,869 victims of the Nazis were buried here. Their graves are known as "Ghetto Field." There are also more than 600 graves of gypsies (in plots P IV & P V) who were either victims of Nazis or typhoid, as well as the common grave of some Polish resistance members.

Though the cemetery served as an execution spot until the very last moment, the Germans did not manage to destroy it.

Indeed, the cemetery survived as the largest Jewish cemetery in Europe, with more than 180,000 monuments. Most of these structures are traditional matzevot, with elaborate symbolic reliefs in the upper parts of the states. Below are epitaphs and unique inscriptions in a square writing, often containing traditional abbreviations, characteristic phrases, and biblical quotations. Some epitaphs, in the style of the eighteenth century, are considerably long, often in the form of an acrostic. On a number of matzevot, a prayer for the dead is inscribed on the back.

Apart from the matzevot, a large quantity of modern monuments, family graves, and mausolea are to be found here, concentrated mainly in the plot along the main alley.

Most styles from the turn of the nineteenth and early twentieth centuries can be seen here: Modernism, Art Nouveau, Neoclassicism, etc. These were crafted by such masters as Hersz Hirszberg, Abraham Ostrzega, Otto Rycher, H. Broder, and L. Pasmanik.

In 1975, some 100 tombstones and monuments were included in the Historical Monuments Register of Lodz; five years later, the entire cemetery was declared a historical monument.

A monument stands in the middle of the cemetery's paved plaza and honors the 200,000 Jews from the greater Lodz area who were murdered by the Nazis. The inscription reads: "To the sacred memory of those who perished in the destruction of the great Jewish community of Lodz and its vicinity. They died a martyr's death at the hands of the Hitlerites in the ghettoes and concentration camps between 1939 and 1945. Your memory will live forever."

Additional plaques have been placed about the cemetery in order to further honor the Shoah victims of Lodz.

Old Jewish Cemetery

It was originally established on Wesola, adjacent to the 1,820 square ells of land that the Jewish community bought from the Lipinski family in 1811. In its present incarnation, the cemetery stands at the intersection of Lutomierska and Zachodonia.

MEMORIALS

Former Gestapo Headquarters

Located on Kimanowskiego, the building now holds a plaque that commemorates Gypsies and the victims of the ghetto.

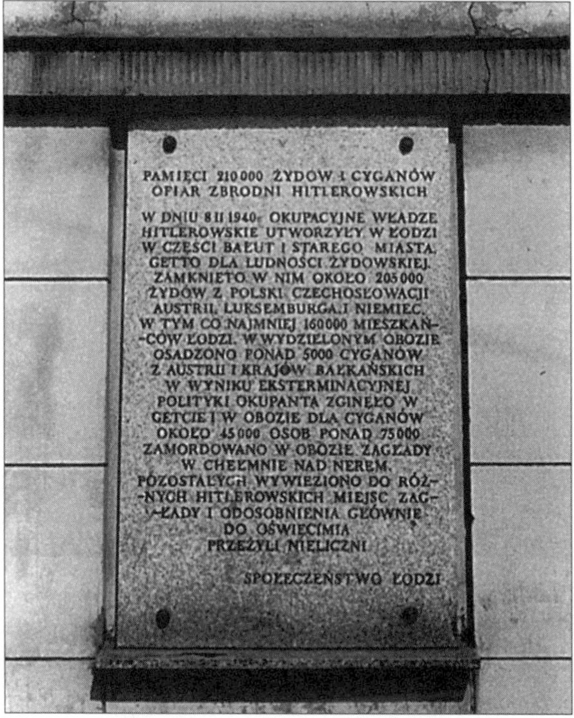

Tablet commemorating the Jews of the Lodz Ghetto.

Perec Playground

This area honors Icchak Leib Perec, the Yiddish writer.

Staromiejski Park

A statue of the Ten Commandments was erected here in 1995 by Gustav Zemla. The project was funded by the Foundation for the Commemoration of the Presence of Jews in Poland.

SECULAR BUILDINGS

Jewish People's Library

Located at 32 Wieckowskiego, it now houses the Jewish Social and Cultural Association.

Jewish State Theater Building

The theater was erected in 1951 on the ruins of the Jewish Scala Theater. Since the Jewish Theater moved its activities to Warsaw, it has been used for general theatrical purposes.

Korczak's Hospital

Located at Armi Czerwonej 15 and Nowa 30, it is named in honor of Janusz Korczak.

Lodz Philharmonic

Named after Artur Rubinstein, it stands at Narutowicza 20.

Poznanski Textile Works

Erected in 1875 at Ogrodowa 17, the building was once owned by the Poznanski Textile Magnates (see mausoleum in New Cemetery).

STREETS

Berlinska

The street was named for Hirsch Berlinski, one of the heroes of the Warsaw Ghetto Uprising.

Julian Tuwima

This thoroughfare is named in honor of Julian Tuwim, a famous Polish-Jewish poet. His name also graces a youth palace (at Moniuszki 4A) and a theater (at Kopernika 8).

SYNAGOGUES

Ulica Rewolucji 1905 No. 20

Built by Rajcher family, this still-active synagogue was destroyed during the war. It was restored to its current condition in 1989.

Ulica Piotrkowska 114/116

The courtyard of the apartment building here served as a printing house and a storage facility after the war. It is currently being renovated.

LUBLIN

The Jewish community here dates back to 1336. It quickly grew, not only in terms of population but in importance as well—a fact underscored by Lublin's nomination as the seat of the Council of the Four Lands (Va'ad Arba Aratzot) in 1581.

By this time, Lublin had also become a vital center of Torah learning, often referred to as the "Jerusalem of Poland." Among the city's most famous Torah scholars were Rabbi Solomon Szachna, the founder of the Talmudic Yeshiva in the sixteenth century; Rabbi Maharshl; Hurwitz Maharam Gedalia Meir; and Yaacov Itzhav Hurvitz Choze (Seer of Lublin).

Other renowned scholars also called Lublin home: Emil Majerson, the philosopher; Zalkind, known as "le Juif de Lublin"; the physicians, Montalo, Vitalis, and Maj; Bela Dobrzycka, the Zionist activist; the writers, Malwina Majerson, Anna Langfus, and Bela Szapiro; Moshe Szulsztajn, the poet; Syncha Trachter, the painter; and the historians, Shalom Baruch Nisenbaum, Bela Mandelsberg, and Szyldkraut.

By the eve of WWII, 40,000 of the 122,000 citizens of the city were Jews, a good number of them employed as grain merchants. Continuing its political heritage, Lublin was an important center of Zionism and all Jewish political parties were active here. The Jewish community also boasted a number of educational establishments: Tarbut high school, Talmud Tora, Beth Yaacov, and Yavneh schools.

The ghetto was established in March 1941. Its exact location was changed a number of times, the final site being Majdan Tatarski. The ghetto was liquidated on November 9, 1942 with the deportation of its inhabitants to Majdanek.

The old Jewish quarter, established in the early sixteenth century around the castle, was entirely destroyed during the occupation.

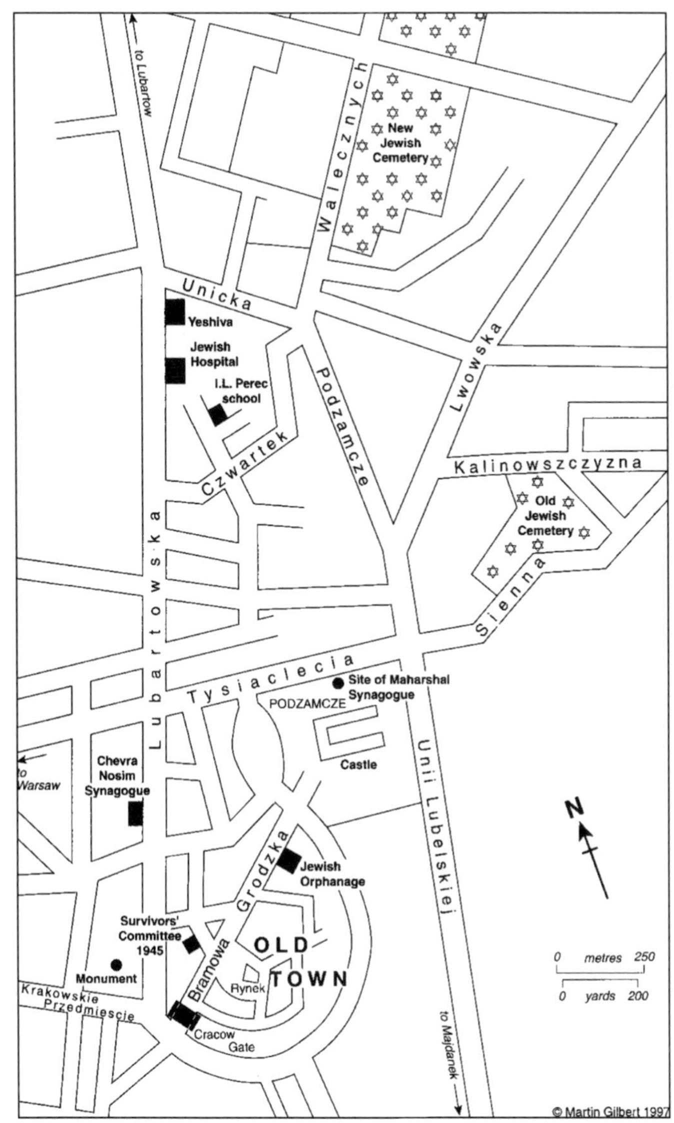

Lublin: Lubartowska Street. Courtesy of Martin Gilbert.

Gravestones and Inscriptions from the Jewish Cemetery in Lublin.

CEMETERIES

Jewish Cemetery

Located at Sienna and Kalinowszczyzna, it was frequently used as an execution site by the Germans. It now contains a tablet honoring these victims of the occupation.

New Jewish Cemetery

The grounds at Ulica Walecznych hold the graves of Holocaust victims who were killed between 1941 and 1942.

A monument here marks the grave of Rabbi Shapiro, the founder of Yeshiva. His remains were reinterred in Jerusalem after the war.

Old Jewish Cemetery (see following map)

This plot contains the graves of many eminent rabbinic authorities, including Solomon Luria (1501–1573, known as "Maharshal"), and Rabbi Meir Lublin (1558–1616, known as "Maharam").

MEMORIALS

Droga Meczennikow Majdanka (Road of the Martyrs of Majdanek)

Located on the road leading from the railway to the camp, a plaque here commemorates the martyrs of Majdanek.

Martyr's Memorial

On the grounds of what was the ghetto, at Ulica Sawicka, the bronze monument marks the spot where Jewish deportees from many countries were assembled before their deportation to the death camps at Leipowa, Majdanek, Plaski, and Sobibor. In doing so, it commemorates the 46,000 Lublin Jews (and 250,000 others) who were murdered by the Nazis.

Buried at the base of the monument are urns that contain the ashes of Jews killed at Belzec, Kremplece, Piniatow, Sobibor, and Zamosc. It bears the following inscription in Polish and Yiddish: "I seek my dear ones in every handful of ashes."

Old Age Home

Located at Ulica Grodzka, it now holds a commemorative tablet.

People's Home

The building on Ulica Perec (named after the writer) is now home to a commemorative tablet on one of its walls.

SECULAR BUILDINGS

Jewish Community Center

Located at Lubartowska 10, the building also serves as a house of worship.

PLAN OF THE OLD JEWISH CEMETERY

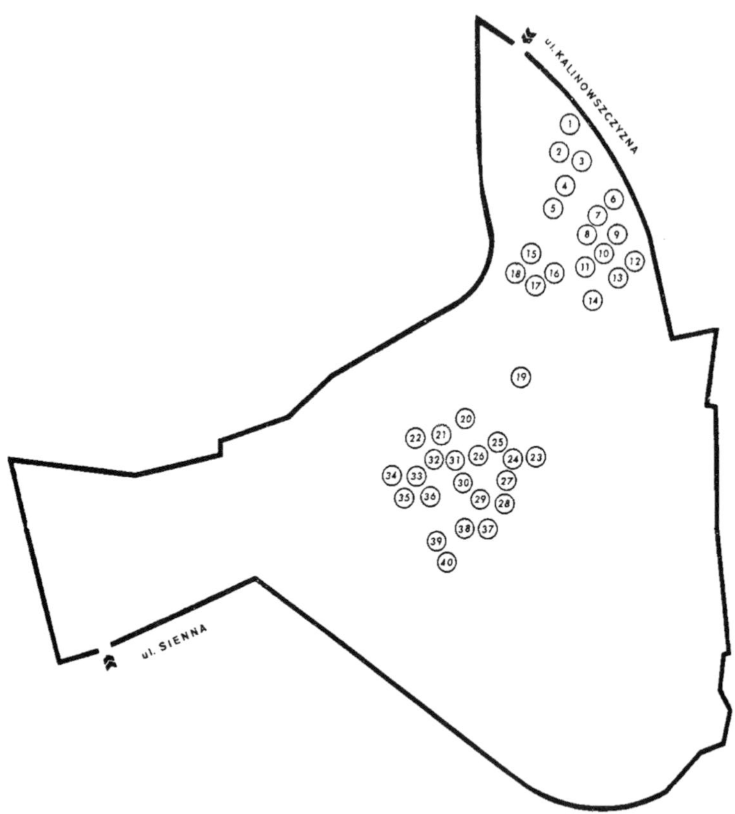

1. Jakow ben Jehuda Halewi Kopelman
2. Hana bat MA
3. Abraham ben Uszaja
4. Jakow Icchak
5. Szloma ben Dawid
6. Jekutiel Zalman
7. Ischar Ber (?)
8. Abraham ben Jakow Iccak Hurwic
9. Miriam bat Szymszon
10. Josef ben Zacharia Mendel
11. Sara Fajga bat Szaul
12. Jehuda Lajib
13. Szalom Szachne ben Josef
14. Dawid Tewi (?) ben Josef
15. Eliezer Lipman (ben Mosze Segal) (?)
16. Jehosza Falk
17. Sara bat Dawid
18. Efraim ben Josef
19. Jakow Dawid ben Mosze
20. Ita bat Menasze Icchak
21. Jehuda bat Mosze Zew
22. Icchak Ajzyk
23. Malka bat Lajb
24. Mosze ben Jehuda
25. Meir ben Meir
26. Heszil ben Jakow
27. Jehuda Lajb ben Meir Aszkenazy
28. Szloma Luria Maharszal
29. Szaul ben Chaim Dawid
30. Jakow ben Efraim Naftali Hirsz
31. Cwi Hirsz ben Zacharia Mendel
32. Meir (?)
33. Natanal ben Meszulam
34. Cwi Hirsz ben Mosze
35. Jakow ben Szmuel
36. Szloma Dawid (Doktor?)
37. Jenta Pesa bar Meir
38. Lea bat Mosze meJanow
39. Zisel bat Szloma
40. Miriam bat Szymon

Jewish Hospital (where author's father worked)

The building at Lubartowska 81 still serves as a medical facility.

Lublin Castle

It now displays the newly restored painting, *Admission of the Jews to Poland*, by Jan Matejko. Commissioned in 1889 by Vienna jurist, Dr. Arnold Rappaport, the painting was presumed lost during the war. However, it resurfaced in the spring of 1967.

Yeshivat Hachamei Lublin

Established in the early twentieth century by Rabbi Meir Shapiro, it was the largest Yeshiva in Poland. Up to 400 students studied there at any given time. The Lublin University School of Medicine now occupies by the building.

A former synagogue on the second floor now serves as the university's auditorium.

SYNAGOGUES

Chevrat Hanoseem

Located on the second floor of an apartment building at Lubartowska 2, it is active whenever a Minyan can be found.

Yeshivat Hachamei in Lublin. Courtesy UJA Archives.

Warsaw Area. Courtesy of Martin Gilbert.

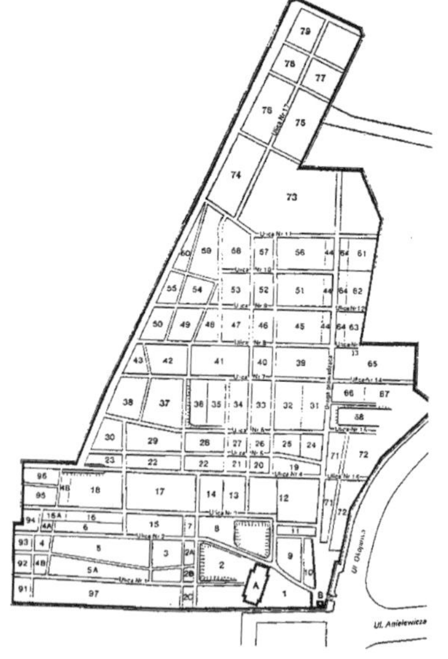

A - Mausoleum of rabbis
B - Prefuneral home
Numerals denote sections

Map of Warsaw Jewish Cemetery.

WARSAW (WARSZAWA)

The first mention of a Jewish presence here dates back to 1414. Famous rabbis of Warsaw include Solomon Zalman Lipszyc, Dov-Ber Meisels, Yaakov Gesundheit, and Chaim Davidson.

All political parties were represented here. A number of newspapers were published even during the occupation, such as *Davar* and *El Al*.

The 390,000 Jewish citizens of 1939 Warsaw made up one-third of the city's total population. The Jewish intelligentsia, industrialists, merchants, craftsmen, and workers had lived here for generations. The political, social, and cultural life of Polish Jews, indeed of European Jewry, was focused in the city.

CEMETERIES

Jewish Cemetery at Brodno

Located in the Prague district across the Wisla River, it was established in 1780 by Szmul Zbytkower (Jozef Samuel Jukubowicz). He donated the land—a plot in what was known as Targowek—after it was bestowed upon him by Stanislaus Augustus Poniatowski, the last king of Poland. Nearly destroyed by the Germans, the cemetery currently contains 300,000 graves. It is being restored under the auspices of the Nissenbaum Foundation.

One well-known person buried here is Abraham Stern, inventor of the mathematical calculating machine.

Polish Army Military Cemetery

Its grounds contain the graves of some Jewish soldiers who were killed in the defense of Warsaw in 1939. An obelisk here, in the form of a matzevot, commemorates 6,500 Jews shot at the sports field, "Skra."

Warsaw Jewish Cemetery

Located at Okopowa 40 at the end of Ulica Anielewicza, it is one of the oldest Jewish historical monuments in Warsaw—established in 1799. The cemetery covers 30 hectares divided into 100 sections, each of which contains 2,000 graves. It is still in use, having miraculously survived the Nazi occupation.

One can find splendid tombstones here, covered with rich ornaments in the shapes of lions, deer, plants, and trees. On the tombs belonging to priestly families (*kohanim*), one can see hands joined in a gesture of blessing; while those of Levite families feature hands holding a jug of water with which priests' hands were sprinkled. A hand throwing a coin into an almsbox is the symbol of a philanthropist, while a hand holding a book appears on the tombs of scholars.

The engravings on the stones are mainly in Hebrew, Yiddish, and Polish with some in Russian and German. Many of the gravestones are the works of renowned sculptors such as Dawid Frydlender, Mieczyslaw Lubelski, Abraham Ostrzega, and Henryk Stifelman.

Some tent (*ohalim*) graves warrant special mention—the "Ohel" of Ber Sonnenberg (son of Szmul Zbytkower), for example. There is also a section of graves that contain Jewish officers and men, soldiers in the Polish army, who were killed during the siege of Warsaw in 1939; a mass grave of 300 unknown Nazi victims; and graves of those who perished in the ghetto, including that of Adam Czerniakow, the president of the Jewish community.

In the cemetery in 1988, Dr. Marek Edelman, the last surviving member of the command of the Warsaw Ghetto

Uprising, dedicated the symbolic grave of Bund leaders Henryk Alter and Viktor Ehrlich. They were councilors of Warsaw who were executed by Stalin for the criticism of the Soviet invasion of Poland in 1939.

The cemetery grounds are currently being restored.

Renowned figures in Polish Jewry Culture buried at the Warsaw Cemetery:

➢ **An-ski, Szymon, 1863–1920**

A student and writer of Jewish folklore, he wrote "Di shvue," which was inspired by the 1905 revolution and came to be the hymn of Jewish socialists. He is best known, however, for the moral drama *Dybuk* (1919), which is still staged around the world. An-ski's collected works were published in 15 volumes in the interwar period.

Section 44, Row 1 (a common grave with J.L. Perec and I. Dinezon).

➢ **Askenazy, Szymon (1867–1935)**

A historian and diplomat, Askenazy was a professor at the University of Lwow from 1904 to 1914. During WWI, he was a member of the committee to assist Polish war victims; from 1920 to 1923, he was First Polish Minister Plenipotentiary to the League of Nations in Geneva.

An expert of eighteenth- and nineteenth-century Polish history, Askenazy also dealt with the history of international relations and diplomacy. His major works were *Ksiaze Jozef Poniatowski*; *Rosja, Polska 1815–1930* (*Russia, Poland 1815–1930*); and *Lukasinski, Napoleon a Polska* (*Napoleon and*

Poland). In all of them, he expresses views on the vitality of the nation, which manifested itself in the stubborn fight for independence.

Askenazy's treatise, *Gdansk a Polska* (1919), persuasively argues Poland's right to the town of Gdansk and its seaport.

Section 10, Row 6.

➢ **Balaban, Majer (1877–1942)**

Balaban was a historian, pedagogue, publicist, and professor at the University of Warsaw; organizer and director of the Rabbinical School in Warsaw; and the coordinator and president of the Institute of Judaic Studies. He popularized the history of Jews, with an emphasis on the history of Jews in Poland.

Balaban wrote in Polish, Yiddish, and Hebrew. His main works include *Dzieje Zydow w Krakowie i na Kazimierzu 1304–1868* (*The History of Jews in Cracow and in Kazimierz 1304–1868*); *Zabytki historyczne Zydow w Polsce* (*Historical Relics of Jews in Poland*); *Bibliografia historii Zydow w Polsce w latach 1900–1930* (*Bibliography of the History of Jews in Poland in the Years 1900–1930*); and a three-volume work entitled *Historia i literatura Zydowska* (*Jewish History and Literature*).

Section 9, Row 10.

➢ **Bergson, Michael (1831–1919)**

A descendant of Szmul Zbytkower, Bergson was a social worker and philanthropist. He served as president of the Community of Orthodox Jews from 1886–1918 and was active in many other social associations, including the Agricultural School for

Youth in Czestoniew. Bergson also founded the Jewish Educational Institutes on Ulica Jagiellonska.
Section 33, Row 10.

➢ **Bersohn, Majer (1787–1873)**
Bersohn was a senior member of a philanthropist and social workers' organization, founder of the children's hospital on Ulica Sliska that bears his name, and founder of a rabbinical school and a Jewish hospital.
Section 26, Row 2.

➢ **Bersohn, Mathias (1824–1908)**
An author of many works on art and culture, Bersohn developed a sizable collection of art and cultural works. Upon his donation of these materials to the Jewish community in 1904, they became the nucleus of the museum of Jewish Antiquities. The remaining collections were later acquired by the National Museum in Warsaw.
Section 26, Row 2.

➢ **Bund Fighters**
There is a collective monument to the ghetto fighters of BUND and CIKUNFT, the youth organization of the party.

➢ **Centnerszwer, Gabriel (1841–1917)**
Centnerszwer was a bookseller, publisher, and participant in the 1863 insurrection. Publisher of more than 200 books, it was on his initiative that the first Polish language primer for Jewish children appeared.

➢ **Czerniakow, Adam (1880–1942)**

In addition to being an engineer and activist, Czerniakow was president of the Central Union of Jewish Craftsmen; senator of the Republic from 1931 to 1935; and chairman of the Jewish Religious Community.

At the time of the occupation (until July of 1942), he served as president of the Council of Elders—an administrative institution formed by the Nazis to execute their orders. On July 22, 1942, Czerniakow was forced by the Gestapo to sign the deportation order of Jews. Realizing that they would be sent to extermination camps, he committed suicide as a sign of protest.

Inscribed on his monument is a fragment of Norwid's composition, "What have you done to Athens?," and Ezekiel 16:6 in Hebrew.

Section 10, Rows 3–4.

➢ **Dickstein, Samuel (1851–1939)**

Dickstein was an author, mathematician, science historian, professor at Warsaw University, and member of scientific societies in Poland and abroad. He also served as the superintendent of the Jewish community's M. Bersohn Museum.

➢ **Eisenbaum, Antoni (1791–1852)**

Director of Warsaw's Rabbinical School, Eisenbaum was also an advocate of the Haskalah Movement. Between 1823 and 1824, he edited *Der Beobachter* and *Der Weichsel*, a German periodical that advocated equal rights for Jews.

Section 1, Row 2.

➢ **Epstein, Jakub (1771–1843)**

Forefather of a known family of industrialists and businessmen, Epstein participated in the Kosciuszko Insurrection in 1794. He was a protector of and contributor to the construction of the Jewish Hospital and synagogue on Danilowiczowska.

Section 9, Row 10.

➢ **Feiner, Leon (1885–1945)**

A lawyer, Feiner was a Bund activist in Cracow before the war. He assumed the pseudonym "Mikolak" during the German occupation, and acted as vice chairman of the Council for Help of Jews (ZEGOTA)—an organization created by the Polish Underground Government to help Jews.

Bund section (Main Alley).

➢ **Frenk, Azriel Natan (1863–1924)**

A publicist and historian, Frenk cooperated with Polish and Hebrew periodicals. He authored the following historical studies: *Wojny Napoleonskie* (*Napoleonic Wars*); *Z przeszlosci zydowstwa warszawskiego* (*From the Past of Warsaw Jewry*); and *Z dziejow cenzury ksiag zydowskich* (*A Contribution to the History of Censorship of Jewish Books*). In addition, Frenk translated Boleslaw Prus' *Faraon* (*The Pharoah*); Sienkiewicz's *Ogniem I Mieczem* (*With Fire and Sword)*; and Sienkiewicz's *Potop* (*The Deluge*) into Yiddish.

Section 44, Row 1.

➢ **Goldkraut, Pawel (1898–1978)**

A civil engineer, Goldkraut served in the Polish Military Organization (P.O.W.) during WWI. After the end of WWII, he participated in the reconstruction of many buildings in Warsaw and in other cities. Among them are the Jewish Theater and Plac Grzybowski, now the seat of the Headquarters of the Social and Historical Society of Jews in Poland. He was also on the Board of Directors of the Jewish Historical Institute.

Section 10, Row 5.

➢ **Goldszmit, Henryk (1878–1942)**

See Korczak, Janusz.

➢ **Kaminska, Estera Rachel (1870–1925)**

Known as the Mother of Jewish Theater, Kaminska made her acting debut in 1888 and went on to perform in many countries. In 1913, she founded the Jewish Theater in Warsaw, naming it after her husband, Abraham Kaminski.

In 1955, the State Jewish Theater in Warsaw was named after her. The monument at her grave was designed by Feliks Rubinlicht.

Section 39, Row 1.

➢ **Klepfisz, Michael (1913–1943)**

An engineer and a leading activist of BUND in the Warsaw Ghetto, Klepfisz was a representative of the Jewish Fighting Organization. He was killed during the Uprising, and is now honored here with a symbolic monument.

Section 20, Main Alley.

➢ **Korczak, Janusz (1878–1942)**

A doctor, educator, and author of children's books, Korczak is best known for *King Matt the First*. Before WWII, he established and ran a Jewish

Janusz Korczak Memorial in the Okopowa Cemetery in Warsaw.

orphanage in Warsaw; edited the children's newspaper, *Maly Przeglad* (*Little Review*); and ran a radio program for children. After declining offers to be rescued, he marched with his children to Umschlagsplatz on August 5, 1942. He subsequently perished in Treblinka. A symbolic monument here was designed by Mieczyslaw Smorczewski and stands parallel to Ulica Okopowa.

Section 72.

➢ **Kramsztyk, Izaak (1814–1889)**

Kramsztyk was a preacher, publicist, and founder of the first reform synagogue in Warsaw (1852). He preached and participated in anti-Russian rallies on the eve of the January Insurrection in 1863. At this time, he appealed for the active solidarity of Jews with the insurgents; for this action, he was exiled into Russia. Kramsztyk later cooperated with Polish papers addressed to the Jewish population, in which he advocated the ideas of progress and tolerance.

Section 20, Row 12.

➢ **Landy, Michael (1844–1861)**

Landy was a participant in the anti-tsarist rally at Plac Zamkowy in Warsaw on April 8, 1861. He was shot the moment he took up a cross that had been held by another protester who fell dead at his side. Landy's death inspired a number of poets and painters—Artur Szyk, among them.

Section 20, Row 12.

➢ **Mark, Bernard (1908–1966)**

Mark was a historian and publicist. In People's Poland, he was an editor of periodicals published by the Social and Cultural Society of Jews in Poland, and director of the Jewish Historical Institute from 1949 to 1966. Mark also wrote about the resistance movement in ghettos, particularly the Warsaw Ghetto Uprising.

Section 64, Row 1.

➢ **Morewski, Abraham (1886–1964)**

Morewski was an actor and stage manager first at the Jewish Theater in Vilna, and later in the United

States. After the Nazi armies invaded the Soviet Union, he acted on Russian stages for approximately twelve years. In 1956, Morewski returned to Poland, where he became one of the leading actors of the Kaminska Theater.

Section 64, Row 1.

➢ **Natanson, Zelig Samuel (1795–1879)**

Patriarch of the Natansons, he was a banker, industrialist, and cofounder of Warsaw's Great Synagogue. Several of his sons played important roles in the cultural and scientific life of Poland.

Section 20, Row 7.

➢ **Orgelbrand, Samuel (1810–1868)**

Orgelbrand was a publisher and bookseller. From 1842 to 1850, he published *Kmiotek* (*Rustic*), the first Polish paper for country people. His crowning achievement, however, was the 28-volume *Encyklopedia Powszechna* (*Universal Encyclopedia*).

Section 20, Row 7.

➢ **Perec, Icchak Leib (1852–1915)**

Perec was a lawyer, dramatist, and writer. After youthful poetic attempts in Polish and Hebrew, he broke through in 1888 with the innovative Yiddish poem "Monisz." He wrote short stories on social problems that were published in the collection *Folksimliche geszichten* (*Country-Folk Tales*). The plot of the Poem "Chsydisz" ("The World of Rabbinists") is based on Orthodox Jewish customs. His dramas *Baj nacht pjfn alten markt* (*By Night on the Old Market Square*) and *Di goldene kajt* (*Golden Chain*) immediately became stock pieces in Jewish theaters around the world.

His numerous novels, satirical pieces, and comprehensive publications—all of which combine modern European thought with Polish national tradition—place Perec among the greats of Yiddish literature.

Section 44, Row 1.

➢ **Perl, Feliks (1871–1927)**

Co-founder of the Polish Socialist Party, Perl was its leading theoretician and publicist. In addition, he was the chief editor of the party's main organ—*Robotnik* (*Worker*)—and a member of the Sejm.

Mieczyslaw Niedzialkowski, celebrated activist of the party, said the following at Perl's grave: "There is no Polish socialist in whom the cause of independence and socialism would be fused to such an extent as in Perl."

Section 24, Row 2.

➢ **Rosenblum-Szymanska, Zofia (1888–1978)**

Rosenblum-Szymanska was a doctor, as well as the co-originator of medical attention stations for children. From 1928 to 1939, she was the head of such a station in Otwock (near Warsaw). In the Warsaw Ghetto, she was the chief doctor of a number of pediatric stations until 1942.

After the liberation, she became head of a dispensary for underdeveloped children at the Institute of Mental Hygiene. She also authored several popular science works and participated in international congresses as a delegate of the Ministry of Health.

Section 67, Row 5.

➢ **Slonimski, Chaim Zelig (1810–1904)**

Slonimski was a mathematician, astronomer, and inventor. He improved the computing machine co-invented by Abraham Stern, his father-in-law. In 1862, he founded the first popular science journal in Hebrew, *Ha-ce-fira* (*Dawn*). He was the grandfather of Anton Slonimski, poet and publicist.

Section 71, Row 1.

➢ **Sonnenberg, Ber (1764–1822)**

Son of Szmul, and popularly known as "Zbytkower," Sonnenberg was a banker, Praga land owner, founder of the Jewish cemetery in that quarter, and a personage cloaked in a mantle of legend dating back to the Kosciuszko Insurrection. In addition, he was a merchant and an entrepreneur.

Descendants of Ber assumed the name of Bergson. One of them, philosopher and writer Henri Bergson, won the Nobel Prize for Literature in 1927.

Section 1, Row 11.

➢ **Wawelberg, Hipolit (1844–1901)**

A financier, philanthropist, and social worker, Wawelberg financed a foundation called "Cheap Apartments in Warsaw," and initiated popular editions of great Polish works. Together with his brother, he founded the High Technical School in 1891, which was incorporated into Warsaw Technical University in 1951. Wawelberg also founded the building that housed the Museum of Industry and Trade.

A street is named after him near the blocks of working-class flats that were financed by his foundation.

Section 20, Row 3.

➢ **Zamenhof, Ludwik (1859–1917)**

An opthalmologist by profession, Zamenhof was the creator of the universal Esperanto language, the first handbook of which appeared in Warsaw in 1887. The main source of inspiration in the creation of Esperanto was the misunderstanding between nationalities in his native city of Bialystok. In the universal language, Zamenhof saw the possibility of making unrestricted contacts between various nationalities. He translated a number of works into Esperanto. Today, approximately 2.5 million people around the world use the language.

His monument was designed by Mieczyslaw Lubelski.

Section 10, Row 2.

GHETTO

Beginning in the middle of 1940, the ghetto walls enclosed Warsaw's Jews, as well as those deported from other areas in Poland and Western Europe. The ghetto's population reached nearly 500,000 people—all of whom lived in terrible conditions and suffered from starvation and disease. Mass deportations began in the summer of 1942, with Treblinka as their destination.

Six months later, with some 60,000 people still in the ghetto, the first Jewish military resistance was organized. This resistance forced the Nazis to retreat and temporarily abandon their ultimate goal: the complete destruction of the ghetto.

On April 19, 1943, an uprising erupted within the ghetto. The resistance fighters from two Jewish groups—the Jewish Combat Organization (Z.O.B.), led by Mordechai Anielewicz, and the Jewish Military Union (Z.Z.W.), led by

Mordechai Anielewicz, commander of the uprising in the Warsaw Ghetto.

Mordechai Tenenbaum—numbered several hundred people. Their well-constructed network of bunkers and defenses was subsequently attacked by more than 2,000 heavily-armed Wehrmacht and SS troops. After a ferocious struggle on May 8, the main bunker at Ulica Mila 18 fell, burying the staff of the Z.O.B. To celebrate their victory, the Nazis blew up the nearby Great Synagogue in Tlomackie on May 16.

In some areas of the ghetto, however, fighting continued until July, during which time some resistance fighters managed to escape through sewers to the Aryan side. The uprising triggered similar actions, though on a smaller scale, in Bialystok, Czestochowa, Bedzin, and Cracow.

In his report to headquarters, Nazi commander Juergen Stroop noted 56,065 Jews captured, 7,000 exterminated, and 5,565 killed in action. The underground Polish press evaluated enemy losses at 400 killed and about 1,000 wounded.

➢ **For a Chronology of the Ghetto, see last the section of the chapter.**

MEMORIALS

"Gdansk" Railroad Station

An exhibit here commemorates the 1968 exodus.

Ghetto Wall Remnants

One set can be found in the courtyard of Zlota 60, near what was known as Ulica Marchlewskiego in the vicinity of the Holiday Inn Hotel. A plaque is affixed to the wall, showing a map of the ghetto.

Another remnant stands on Ulica Sienna (Little Ghetto).

The Grave of the Unknown Soldier

Located at Plac Zwyciestwa, across the street from the Victoria Hotel, it lists the Warsaw Ghetto Uprising among the major battles fought during World War II.

Kopciowka in Wilanow

A plaque here commemorates 67 Jews who were shot in May 1944.

Memory Lane

Erected on the forty-fifth anniversary of the Warsaw Ghetto Uprising, this series of stone markers stand along the path from the Warsaw Ghetto Uprising Monument to Zygelbojm Square, Mila 18, and Umschlagsplatz (all described below). These markers elucidate, in Polish and Hebrew, various facets of the fight and martyrdom of the Warsaw Jews. Designed by Z. Gasior and S. Jankowski, Memory Lane is comprised of the following commemorations:

1. **Memory Tree**
2. **Creation of the ghetto in 1940**

Tomb of Unknown Soldier lists the participants in the Warsaw Ghetto Uprising.

3. **Ghetto Uprising** from April 19 to May 15, 1943
4. **Emmanuel Ringelblum**
5. **Jozef Lewartowski**, Socialist party activist executed in 1942 and posthumously awarded the Grunwald Cross.
6. **Michael Klepfisz**, Bund activist killed in action on the second day of the Uprising and posthumously awarded Virtuti Militari
7. **Szmuel Zygelbojm**
8. **Szmuel Zygelbojm** (II)
9. **Arieh Wilner**, Hashomer Hatzair activist and liaison officer between the Polish and Jewish Undergrounds, who perished with the command, and was posthumously awarded Virtuti Militari
10. **Mordechai Anielewicz**, member of Hashomer Hatzair and commander of Z.O.B.—the Jewish Combat Organization; leader of the Uprising who committed suicide, with the rest of his command, on May 8, 1943 at Mila 18, and who was posthumously awarded Virtuti Militari
11. **Meir Majerowicz**, "Marek," member of Poalei Zion, who was posthumously awarded the Cross of Valor
12. **Frumka Plotnicka**, liaison officer between Jewish underground units in Warsaw, Sosnowiec, and Bedzin, who was killed in action and posthumously awarded the Grunwald Cross
13. **Rabbi Itzhak Nyssenbaum**, leader of religious Zionists and member of the underground ghetto organization, who perished in Treblinka
14. **Janusz Korczak**, educator, physician, and writer who perished with the children of his orphanage, whom he would not abandon
15. **Ichak (Itzhak) Katzenelson**, Hebrew and Yiddish poet and author of *The Song about the Murdered Jewish Nation*, who perished in Auschwitz

16. At **Stawki 5/7**, building that housed the SS command of the Umschlagplatz, which oversaw the deportation of ghetto inhabitants to Treblinka
17. At **Stawki 6/8**, building that housed the school and temporary hospital where Jews were held before deportation

Plaque on Memory Lane at the Jewish Hospital.

Stone slab on the site where the Jewish Combat Organization bunker was hidden.

Mila Eighteen

The building here housed the bunker where Anielewicz and his commanders met their deaths. A modest memorial exists here in the form of a mound and an inscribed monument: "On this spot on May 8, 1943, Mordechai Anielewicz, commander of the Warsaw Uprising, met a Soldier's Death, together with the rest of the command of the Jewish Combat Organization in their struggle against German occupiers."

Monument to Soldiers of the Polish Army

It honors all those who fell in the defense of Warsaw in 1939. Of the one million Polish Army members who fought the German invasion, approximately 100,000 were Jews. According to historian Filip Friedman, 32,000 were killed in action, while 61,000 were captured.

Polish Underground Plaque

Located at Anielewicza 34, it commemorates the Polish Underground's liberation of 348 Jewish prisoners from the German Concentration camp "Gesiowska." Many of its members fought and fell during the Warsaw Uprising.

Praga-Polnoc

At the southern railroad station, a plaque commemorates 600 Jews who were murdered by the Germans.

Umschlagplatz

The house next to this infamous spot, where Nazis made their "selections" for deportations, bears three simple plaques. Affixed to the wall on Ulica Stawki, they tell the tragic history of the location in Polish, Hebrew, and Yiddish.

Memorial on the site of the former Umschlagplatz.

A full-scale memorial is to be erected at the present site of a gas station. The first phase of the project—designed by Hanna Szmalenberg and Wladyslaw Klamerus—was completed in April 1988 to coincide with the forty-fifth anniversary of the

Uprising. First names of Polish Jews are engraved on the monument's walls in a fashion similar to the Vietnam War Memorial. The inscription above them reads: "Along this path of suffering and death, over 300,000 were driven in 1942/1943 from the Warsaw Ghetto to the gas chambers of the Nazi extermination camps.

Warsaw Ghetto Uprising Monument

Located at Anielewicza and Zamenhof, it stands on the site of the Central Command Post, where the first shots were fired at dawn on April 19, 1943. Designed by Natan Rapaport, the 36-foot monument consists of a bronze statue group mounted in front of a towering granite wall. (The granite had originally been ordered by Hitler's sculptor, Arno Breker, for a projected victory monument.) The inscription—in Polish, Hebrew, and Yiddish—reads: "The Jewish People—to its Heroes, and its Martyrs."

A circular memorial in the area marks the manhole cover used by the ghetto fighters. It was the first memorial, erected on the fifth anniversary of the Uprising.

Monument of the Heroes of Warsaw Ghetto, by N. Rapaport. Courtesy of D. Goldberg.

Wilanow

On the road to Powsina, an obelisk honors 67 Jews shot in May 1944.

Wola

At the Jewish cemetery wall at Ulica Mlynarska 68, a plaque commemorates 68 Jews who were shot in August 1944.

Zamenhof Memorial

On the building at Zamenhof 5, a plaque honors Dr. Ludwik Zamenhof, the Bialystok physician who invented Esperanto in 1887. The plaque was dedicated on the centennial of his birth (1959) by the International Congress of Esperantists, in order to replace the 1928 monument that had been destroyed by the Nazis.

Zamenhof lived in Warsaw for most of his adult life and is buried at the Warsaw Cemetery, where groups of Esperantists regularly visit his grave.

Zegota Memorial

In honor of the Relief Council for Jews, it was erected near the Warsaw Ghetto Monument by the American Friends. It was designed by Hanna Szmalenberg and Marek Moderav.

ZEGOTA (Council Aid for Jews) was the only organization of its kind in German-occupied Poland that exclusively aided Jews with funds provided by its government. Zegota considered Jewish housing a basic, if not the most important form of aid because the life of a Jew depended upon a place to live. Since Germans executed Poles for contact with Jews and extended the death penalty to the offender's entire family, including children, the primary obstacle facing Zegota operatives was the natural fear of

Poles about sheltering Jews. Zegota distributed 50,000 forged documents, of which 80% reached Jewish hands. At least 40,000 to 50,000—or about half of the Jews who survived the Holocaust in German-occupied Poland—benefitted from some form of aid from Zegota.

Zygelbojm Memorial

Designed by Marek Moderav, it was unveiled in 1988 at the corner of Lewandowskiego and Zamenhofa. On an office building here, a memorial plaque hangs in honor of Szmuel Zygelbojm.

MUSEUMS

Jewish Historical Institute

The Martyr's Museum is located here (see page 187).

National Archeological Museum

Located at Dluga 53, the museum's paintings department contains a collection of Judaica, as well as paintings and engravings with Jewish themes.

SECULAR BUILDINGS

Jewish Academic House

On Ulica Sierakowskiego 7 in the Praga section, it is presently used for local government offices. The acronym AAJ—Auxilium Academicum Judaicum—are still visible on the building's exterior.

Jewish Community Headquarters

Located in a compound of sorts at Twarda 6, the building houses a kosher kitchen, a mikvah, a synagogue, a theater, and a cultural association. It also serves as the national headquarters of the Union of Jewish Religious Communities. All of the social work here is supported by the American Joint Distribution Committee.

Jewish Cultural House

Located at Plac Grzybowski 3, it was established in 1966. The building houses the Jewish Cultural-Social Association, a Jewish cooperative, the Yiddish State Theater (see below), and the editorial offices of *Folks-Sztym*—Poland's only Jewish newspaper published in both Polish and Yiddish.

Jewish Historical Institute

Located at Aleje Swierczewskiego 79, the institute was established in 1949 at the prewar site of the Judaic Institute and Central Library. It functions under the auspices of the Polish Academy of Sciences. Its hours of operation are Monday through Friday from 9 A.M. to 3 P.M., and Saturday from 9 A.M. to noon.

Jewish Historical Institute in Warsaw.

The institute carries out scientific research on the history of Jews in Poland, as well as in other countries. The results of its studies are published in books and in *The Bulletin of the Jewish Historical Institute*, a quarterly publication in Polish with English and Yiddish summaries. It also publishes a Yiddish magazine entitled *Bletter far Geszichte* (*Pages of History*).

The institute boasts a library of more than 50,000 volumes that treat Judaic and Semetic subjects—many old and unique publications among them. Some of the collected manuscripts date from the tenth century, while a collection of Jewish newspapers from the nineteenth century is also available.

In addition, the institute's holdings include rare records of ancient Jewish communities, documents dealing with the Nazi occupation and Jewish martyrdom, and files collected by Emanuel Ringelblum during his activities in the underground resistance movement.

Dr. Ringelblum, a historian by profession, organized an underground archive code-named "Oneg-Shabbat" in the early 1940s. The documents describe the life and events of the Warsaw Ghetto from 1939 to 1943. Buried inside milk cans behind a concrete-reenforced door to avoid their discovery by the Germans, they were found only in 1946 and 1950. Now, this collection stands as the most important part of the permanent exhibition.

The Judaica collection was assembled from the remnants of Jewish Yeshivot, museums, libraries, and theological seminaries that had been looted by the Nazis throughout Europe. Abandoned in a long line of freight cars in Silesia, the rescued materials include manuscripts, books, and documents. Among the rare items on exhibit are a ninth-century parchment diary of a Jewish traveler to Poland; a letter from Spinoza's teacher; contemporary records of the Sabbatai Zvi messianic movement in the seventeenth century; the minutes of the Council of the Four Lands in the seventeenth century; and Jewish communal archives from many Polish and Silesian towns.

The two upper floors, known as the *Martyrs' Museum*, are entirely devoted to the story of the Warsaw Ghetto and other Polish ghettos. The most unusual exhibit consists of the rusty milk cans of Dr. Emanuel Ringelblum. Above the cans hangs a portrait of the historian, who was shot by the Nazis after the ghetto's destruction. Another can contains an old hunting rifle and two pistols, part of the weaponry employed by the ghetto fighters.

Elsewhere in the museum are the records of the Jewish Councils established by the Nazis; files of ghetto newspapers, execution orders, and statistics of arrivals and departures from the Warsaw Ghetto; the files of the Warsaw branch of the JDC up until December of 1941; and a large gallery of photographs and paintings that depict life in the Warsaw Ghetto. Also on exhibition are portraits of WWII statesmen and leaders such as Dr. Chaim Weizmann, Moshe Sharett, David Ben-Gurion, Stalin, Churchill, Roosevelt, and Eisenhower.

On the thirty-fifth anniversary of the Uprising, an exhibition entitled "Art and Culture behind the Walls" was created to recognize the talents of murdered artists such as, Adolf Behrman, Jakub Glasner, Henryk Glicenstein, Marcin Kitz, Jozef Kowner, Roman Kramsztyk, Mojzesz Rynecki, Bruno Schultz, Efraim and Menasze Seidenbeutlow, Geli Seksztajn, Jonasz Stern, and Maurycy Trebacz.

Korczak Orphanage

Located at Ulica Jaktorowka 8, it is named in honor of Dr. Janusz Korczak, a small statue of whom stands in the courtyard. Affixed to the building itself are two plaques: one honors Korczak, while the other honors the Polish janitor of the orphange, Piotr Zalewski, who was shot by the Nazis in 1944.

Lauder-Morasha School

Previously located in a rented building, it moved in October 1999 to a completely renovated and well-equipped

Statue at the Korczak Orphanage.

building at Wawelberga 10. (Before the war, the building served as an old age home.) When the school first opened under the auspices of the Lauder Foundation, it instructed only 15 students. Now it serves to ten times that number.

Yiddish State Theater

Before moving to New York in 1968, Ida Kaminska made the Jewish theater at Plac Grzybowski 3 famous with her star performances and productions. Interrupted for the duration of the war, it was revived immediately after the liberation of Lodz.

The theater moved to Wroclaw in 1949 to serve the city's large Jewish population of the time, when a new theater opened in Lodz. The two theaters merged in 1950 as the State Jewish Theater, which was named after Ida's mother, Esther Kaminska. Five years later, it permanently moved to Warsaw.

Subsequently, a number of personalities here became famous throughout the Jewish theatrical world: Ida Kaminska, Abraham Morewski, Chewel Buzgan, Juliusz Berger, Mieczylaw Bram, Adam Czarka, Seweryn Dalecki, Piotr Erlich, Estera Kowalska, Herman Lercher, Jakub Rotbaum, Szymon Szurmiej, Michal Szweklich, and Tywa Szyler-Buzgan.

Since 1970, the theater has been under the management of Szymon Szurmiej, the leading actor of the theater and a former member of the Sejm.

STREETS

Anielewicza

This stretch is named after Mordechai Anielewicz, commander of the Jewish Combat Organization. He was barely 20 when Soviet authorities arrested him in 1939 for organizing the emigration of Jews from Russian-occupied areas of Poland to Palestine. Upon his release one year later, Anielewicz became the leader of Jewish underground groups in Vilna and Czestochowa. Two years later, he was appointed commander-in-chief of the Jewish Combat Organization.

During the heroic struggle of Jews against the Nazis, he and the members of his command committed suicide rather than fall into German hands.

Here follows Mordechai Anielewicz's last letter:

> The last wish of my life has been fulfilled.
>
> It is now clear to me that what took place exceeded all expectations. In our opposition to the Germans, we

did more than our strength allowed but now our forces are waning. We are on the brink of extinction. We forced the Germans to retreat twice, but they returned stronger than before.

One of our groups held out for forty minutes; and another fought for about six hours. The mine that was laid in the area of the brush factory exploded as planned. Then we attacked the Germans and they suffered heavy casualties. Our losses were generally low. That is an accomplishment, too. Z. fell, next to his machine gun.

I feel that great things are happening and that this action that we have dared to take is of enormous value.

We have no choice but to go over to partisan methods of fighting as of today. Tonight, six fighting groups are out. They have two tasks: to reconnoiter the area and to capture weapons. Remember, short-range weapons are of no use to us. We employ them very rarely. We need many rifles, hand grenades, machine guns, and explosives.

I cannot describe the conditions in which the Jews of the ghetto are now "living." Only a few exceptional individuals will be able to survive such suffering. The others will sooner or later die. Their fate is certain, even though thousands are trying to hide in cracks and rat holes. It is impossible to light a candle for lack of air. Greetings to you who are outside. Perhaps a miracle will occur, and we shall see each other again one of these days. It is extremely doubtful.

The last wish of my life has been fulfilled. Jewish self-defense has become a fact. Jewish resistance and revenge have become actualities. I am happy to have been one for the first Jewish fighters in the ghetto.

Where will rescue come from?

Fundamanskiego

This street honors the memory of Ephraim Fundamanski, one of the organizers of the Warsaw Ghetto Uprising.

Lewartowska

Located between Gesia and Anielewicza, it memorializes Joseph Lewartowski, one of the leaders of the ghetto underground.

Pereca

Formerly Ulica Ceglana, it now honors Icchak Lieb Perec, who lived in Warsaw from 1887 until his death in 1915. His Yiddish stories and poems describe the hardships of Jewish life in the Eastern European shtetl.

Skwer Zygelbojma

Located between the Ghetto Memorial and Mila 18, the square is named after Szmuel Zygelbojm, member of the Polish National Council (Parliament-in-Exile) in London. At the end of the Warsaw Ghetto Uprising, he committed suicide to protest the world's indifference.

Following are excerpts from his final letter and testament:

> I Cannot Keep Silent and
> Cannot Continue to Live.
>
> Mr. President, Mr. Premier,
>
> I take the liberty to address my last words to you and through your intermediary to the Polish government and Polish people, to the governments and peoples of Allied nations, to the conscience of the world. . . .
>
> I cannot keep silent and cannot continue to live when the remnants of the Jewish people in Poland, whom I represent, are perishing.

Our comrades in the Warsaw Ghetto lost their lives, fighting with arms in hand, in a last heroic rising. I was not given the opportunity to perish as they did, together with them. But I belong to them, and should share their mass grave.

My death is to serve as the deepest protest against the passivity with which the world looks at all this and permits the annihilation of the Jewish people. I know how little human life means, especially today. But since I was unable to achieve it during my lifetime, perhaps my death will help to shatter the indifference of those who could and should do something about it, so that now, at the very last moment, that handful of Polish Jews who are still alive can be saved from extermination.

My life belongs to the Jewish people in Poland, that is why I sacrifice it. It is my desire that this handful that remains of the several-million strong Polish Jewry, can together with the Polish masses look forward to liberation, can breathe the air of freedom and justice of socialism in Poland and the world for all the inhuman torments they have suffered. And I believe that precisely such a Poland and such a world will arise. . . .

[*Excerpts from the letter and testament addressed to Wladyslaw Raczkiewicz, President of the Polish Republic, and General Wladyslaw Sikorski, premier of the government-in-exile of the Polish Republic, which had its headquarters in London.*]

Szterna

It is named in honor of Abraham Sztern, a pioneer of the Haskalah Movement in Poland, director of the rabbinical seminary, and inventor of an early nineteenth-century adding machine.

SYNAGOGUES

Great Synagogue on Tlomackie

Warsaw's most famous synagogue was designed by Leandro Marconi not after classic Hassidic models, but rather those of Oranienburgerstrasse (Berlin) and St. Charles Borromeo (Vienna). The synagogue's construction lasted several years, with the inauguration ceremony occurring in 1878.

Accommodating slightly more than 1,100 persons, it served the more assimilated inhabitants of Warsaw—a fact attested to by Rabbi Samuel Poznanski's translation of the prayerbook into Polish.

Following the Warsaw Ghetto Uprising, Nazi troops under the command of General Stroop blew up the synagogue on May 16, 1943.

A detailed model of the Tlomackie synagogue has recently been put on display at Beth Hatefutzot in Tel Aviv.

Grozdowski, The Synagogue on Tlomackie Street in Warsaw, *wood engraving.*

Nozyk Synagogue

Located at Twarda 6, it is named in honor of Rywka and Manasse Nozyk. Their son, Zalman, bought the plot in 1893 with the intention of founding a synagogue upon it. Five years later, the construction finally began and lasted for four years. Zalman personally paid for the entire (and exceedingly expensive) cost of construction—250,000 roubles.

The religious opening of the synagogue occurred on May 12, 1902, on Lag ba-Omer. Owing to the architectural similarities between the Nozyk and Great Synagogues—neo-Romanesque style with neo-Byzantine stucco ornaments—it is speculated that the Nozyk was also designed by Leandro Marconi. Tradition, however, bestows the honor upon Prechner.

During the occupation, the synagogue was used for stabling and fodder storage, thereby causing considerable damage. Bombardments of the city during the Uprising caused further damage to the roof and upper stories. In the late 1940s, it was roughly reconstructed and put to religious use.

Nozyk Synagogue in Warsaw.

A thorough reconstruction took place from 1977 to 1983 under the supervision of architects Hanna Szczepanowska and Eva Dziedzic. At this time, new quarters for the Religious Union of the Mosaic Faith in the Polish People's Republic were attached to the eastern wall. The official reopening occurred on April 18, 1983.

After years of absence, a rabbi now officiates at the Nozyk Synagogue. Rabbi Menachem Joskowitz, an Israeli import, arrived in 1989. His presence has been supported by the Lauder Foundation.

The synagogue has been seeing a renaissance with large attendances at monthly concerts of recorded *hazzanut*, the songs of the famed cantors. As many as 700 people regularly attend these concerts.

As a historical monument, the synagogue is open to the public on Thursdays from 10 A.M. to 3 P.M.

Old Synagogue

Once situated on the corner of Szeroka and Petersburska (now Wojcika and Jagielonska), it was built in 1840 after Jozef Lessel's design. It survived until 1939. Devastated during the war, it was to be reconstructed; however, it was thoughtlessly and hastily demolished.

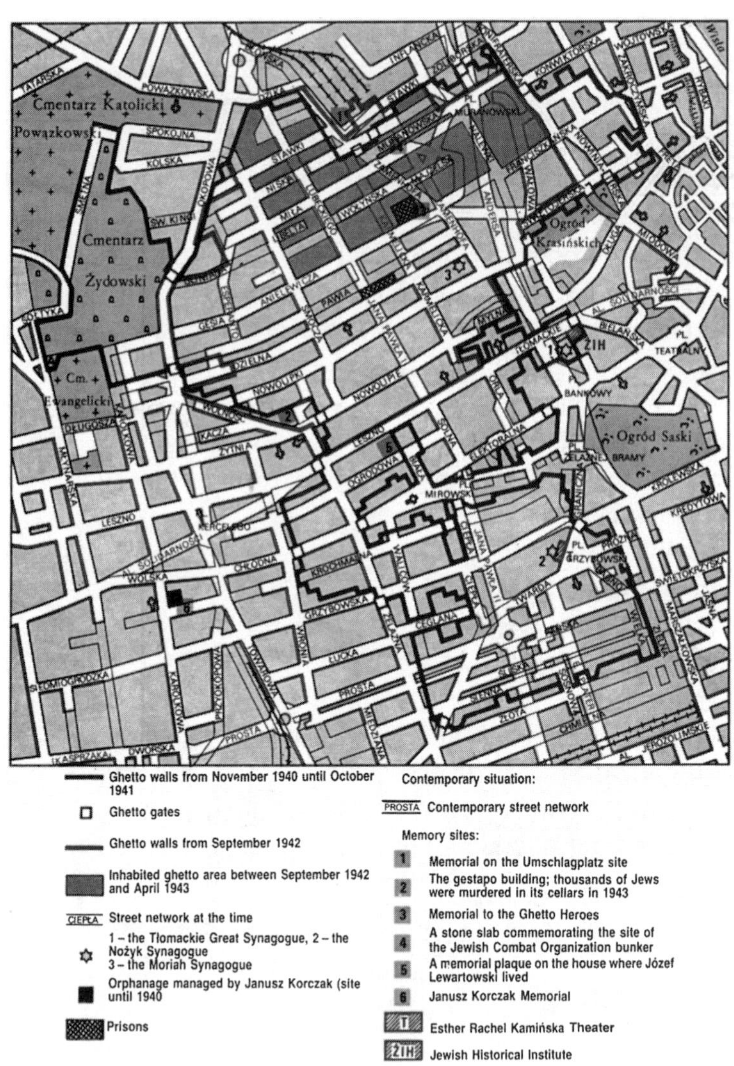
Ghetto walls from November 1940 until October 1941
Ghetto gates
Ghetto walls from September 1942
Inhabited ghetto area between September 1942 and April 1943
CIEPŁA Street network at the time
1 – the Tłomackie Great Synagogue, 2 – the Nożyk Synagogue
3 – the Moriah Synagogue
Orphanage managed by Janusz Korczak (site until 1940
Prisons
Contemporary situation:
PROSTA Contemporary street network
Memory sites:
1 Memorial on the Umschlagplatz site
2 The gestapo building; thousands of Jews were murdered in its cellars in 1943
3 Memorial to the Ghetto Heroes
4 A stone slab commemorating the site of the Jewish Combat Organization bunker
5 A memorial plaque on the house where Józef Lewartowski lived
6 Janusz Korczak Memorial
T Esther Rachel Kamińska Theater
ŻIH Jewish Historical Institute
Cmentarz Katolicki Powązkowski
Cmentarz Żydowski
Cm. Ewangelicki
Ogród Krasińskich
Ogród Saski

The Warsaw Ghetto.

Chronology of the Warsaw Ghetto

Outside Warsaw	Warsaw
1939	
<u>August</u> Germany and Soviet Union sign a non-aggression pact, giving Germany a free hand in Poland.	
<u>9–1</u> Germany invades Poland. (The Polish-Jewish population numbers 3,351,000 and suffers tremendous losses during the German invasion. In Warsaw alone, 30% of Jewish-affiliated buildings are destroyed, and 32,216 Jewish soldiers are killed. Privates Dawid Wachmeister and Lejb Katz are awarded "Virtuti Militari"—the Polish equivalent of the Congressional Medal of Honor.) The SS and Wehrmacht instigate numerous executions.	
<u>9–17</u> Soviet troops invade and occupy Eastern Poland.	

Outside Warsaw	1939 Warsaw
9–21 Reinhardt Heydrich, chief of German Security Police, plans ghettos in Poland.	
	9–27 Warsaw surrenders.
September Germany and the Soviet Union partition Poland into three parts: one incorporated into the German Reich; one to Soviet Union; and one under a German protectorate (Government General). Jewish star introduced.	
	10–4 Adam Czerniakow ordered by Gestapo to form Jewish Council within 24 hours.
10–6 Hitler announces his resettlement policy, including Jewish isolation.	
10–8 Decree reincorporating pre-1918 German	

Outside Warsaw	1939 Warsaw
provinces, as well as Lodz, into the German Reich.	
10–12 First deportation of Jews from Vienna and Bohemia to Nisko in Poland.	
10–26 Forced labor imposed on all Jews living in Government General.	
10–28 First ghetto established in Piotrkow Trybunalski. Jewish badge, Star of David, imposed at Wroclawek.	
	November Census shows 359,827 Jews in the city.
11–8 Hans Frank made Governor General of Poland. Attempt to assassinate Hitler in Munich.	

Outside Warsaw	1939/1940 Warsaw
11–15 Germans forced to readmit Jews formerly deported across Soviet lines as part of a German-Soviet agreement.	
11–23 Jewish badge made compulsory throughout Government General.	
11–30 Soviet Union attacks Finland.	
12–28 The Lodz Ghetto established.	
1940	
January Jendrzejew Ghetto established.	
	1–21 Gestapo orders registration of Jewish property.

Outside Warsaw	1940	Warsaw
		<u>1–26</u> Congregational worship forbidden; ritual slaughter prohibited.
<u>March</u> Czestochowa Ghetto established.		
<u>3–12</u> Soviet Union makes peace with Finland.		
<u>April</u> Deblin Ghetto established.		
<u>4–9</u> Germany invades Denmark and Norway.		
<u>4–14</u> Frank declares that Cracow will be "free of Jews."		
<u>4–30</u> First enclosed and guarded ghetto set up in Lodz.		
<u>5–6</u> Ghetto established at Siedlce.		

Outside Warsaw	1940 Warsaw
5–10 Germany invades Belgium, Holland, and France.	
5–15 Holland surrenders.	
5–28 British evacuate Dunkirk.	
June Tomaszow Ghetto established. First issue of Jewish newspaper.	Jewish Council limited to carrying out German orders.
6–10 Italy enters war.	
6–20 Hitler mentions plan to resettle European Jewry on the island of French Madagascar.	
6–21 France signs armistice with Germany.	
7–12 Frank claims to have persuaded Hitler to stop deporting Jews to the Government General.	

Outside Warsaw	1940	Warsaw
7–19 Hitler offers peace to England.		
August Plonsk Ghetto established.		
September Ghetto at Zdunska established.		Quarantine area, later the ghetto, contains 240,000 Jews and 80,000 Christians.
10–4 French Vichy Government's Jewish Statute deprives refugee Jews of their civil rights.		
10–5 German troops invade Romania.		
		10–16 Decree gives Christians two weeks to move from quarantine area; and Jews two weeks to move in.
November Wroclawek Ghetto established.		

Outside Warsaw	1940/1941	Warsaw
		11–15 Warsaw Ghetto sealed off.
1941		
		January Jewish Council census reports 378,979 Jews in ghetto.
1–11 Frank obtains postponement of plans to deport all Jews to the Government General.		
1–22 Iron Guard revolt in Romania.		
1–31 First attempt to create a Jewish Council in France.		
		Febuary–April 72,000 Jews deported to the ghetto.
2–17 Romania enters war allied with Germany.		

Outside Warsaw	1941	Warsaw
		2–18 Jewish Council granted a loan from German banks, using blocked Jewish accounts as collateral.
2–22 Deportation of Jewish hostages from Amsterdam.		
March Ghetto established at Cracow.		
3–1 Bulgaria enters war allied with Germany.		
3–2 Hitler outlines plans for invasion of Russia to his generals.		
3–4 Construction of Bunawerk factory at Auschwitz authorized.		
3–30 Vichy Government appoints the Commission on Jewish Questions.		

Outside Warsaw	1941	Warsaw
3–30 (cont.) British troops land in Greece.		
		April Schools licensed for 5,000 of the 50,000 children in the ghetto. JDC allowed offices in the city.
4–6 Germans invade Yugoslavia and Greece.		
		May Census cites 430,000 Jews.
5–14 3,600 naturalized Parisian Jews interned.		
5–15 Petain broadcasts pledge of cooperation with Germany.		
End May Einsatzgruppen, or special extermination squads formed.		

Outside Warsaw	1941	Warsaw
June 28 German-inspired pogroms at Kovno, Lithuania.		
6–22 Germany invades Russia.		
6–25 Romanian pogrom at Jassy.		
		July 17,800 refugees—3,300 children, among them—classified as destitute.
		August 3,000 Jews employed in cooperative workshops.
Mid-August Puppet Slovak government disperses Bratislava Ghetto.		
		September Frank announces a reduction in ghetto rations. Post office forbidden to handle foreign mail.

Outside Warsaw	1941 Warsaw
9–1 Massacre of Hungarian Jews at Kamenets-Podolski.	
9–15 Slovakia adopts Nuremberg Laws. Jewish badge declared throughout Greater Reich.	
9–19 Germans occupy Kiev. Zhitomir Ghetto in Ukraine liquidated.	
9–23 Experimental gassing at Auschwitz.	
9–28 Massacre of 34,000 Jews from Kiev.	
October Vast massacres at Riga, Vilna, Kovno, and Dvinsk.	Streetcar lines abolished.
10–2 Paris synagogues blown up by Gestapo.	

Outside Warsaw	1941 Warsaw
	<u>10–5</u> Death edict for leaving ghetto without permission and for sheltering or hiding Jews.
<u>10–12</u> Moscow partially evacuated.	
<u>10–20</u> First deportation from Reich decreed (to Lodz).	
	<u>10–23</u> Liquidation of the small ghetto.
<u>10–29</u> First Jewish inmates arrive at Buna Camp in Auschwitz (owned by I.G. Farben Company).	
	<u>11–4</u> Lodz deportations completed.
<u>11–6</u> 15,000 massacred at Rovno. First Reich Jews arrive in Riga, Minsk, and Kovno.	

Outside Warsaw	1941	Warsaw
End November First massacre at Rostov. Threat to Moscow over.		
		December Jewish cemetery walled off; coffins used for smuggling. Free soup kitchens support 100,000 people.
		12–1 Receipt of food packages forbidden under pretense of epidemic prevention.
12–7 Riga Massacre concluded.		Pearl Harbor bombing leads to withdrawal of JDC.
12–11 Germany declares war on United States.		
12–16 Frank reports that about 2.5 million Jews in Government General must be "gotten rid of."		
		12–17 German post office refuses to accept ghetto mail with the excuse of epidemics.

Outside Warsaw	Warsaw
12–22 Vilna Massacre completed.	
12–30 Crimea Massacres concluded.	
12–31 First permanent gassing camp opened at Chelmno.	
1942	
	January Visits and tours of ghetto ineffectively abolished for German soldiers on leave.
1–15 Resettlement operation begins in Lodz.	
1–20 The Wannsee Conference sets the stage for the Holocaust.	
1–31 Total of 229,052 Jews reported killed in Baltic States and White Russia. First deportation to Teresienstadt.	

Outside Warsaw	1942	Warsaw
2–15 Singapore falls.		
3–15 Hitler promises annihilation of Russia by summer.		
3–16 Belzec death camp opens.		
		4–12 Rumored arrival of extermination brigade.
4–14 News of Lublin Ghetto massacre. News of pogroms in provinces.		
		4–18 Bloody Friday execution of printers and distributors of undercover press. (Ringelblum blames Kohn and Heller.)
4–26 Reichstag approves Hitler's abrogation of German law.		

Outside Warsaw	**1942** **Warsaw**
	May The "Thirteen" gang of collaborators killed.
5–31 First large-scale air raids of Germany (at Cologne).	
June News of massacres at Pabianice and Biala Podlaska.	
6–1 Jewish badge decreed in France and Holland.	
6–23 First gas chamber selection occurs at the train ramp at Birkenau.	
July Massacres extend to Minsk, Lida, Slonim, and Rovno.	
7–1 Germans reach El Alamein (Egypt) and the Don River (Russia).	

Outside Warsaw	1942	Warsaw
		7–22 A total of 380,000 inhabitants. The Jewish Council publishes notice of deportation to the East, regardless of sex or age. In protest, Czerniakow takes his own life.
		7–29 Meeting of Zionist youth organizations to create a unified striking force.
		July Zygmunt returns with proof of extermination at Treblinka.
August Hans Frank: "1.2 million Jews will no longer be provided with food."		
8–4 First deportation train from Belgium to Auschwitz.		
		8–5 Extermination squad arrives. The operation lasts a week.

Outside Warsaw	1942 Warsaw
	8–7 Blockade of every house and street begins.
8–10 to 8–22 40,000 Jews resettled from Lwow.	
Mid-August Germans in north Caucasus.	
8–19 Allies raid Dieppe.	
	8–20 Jozef Szerynski, head of the Jewish police, badly wounded by an attacker.
8–26 Roundup of 7,000 stateless Jews in Vichy.	
9–16 Lodz resettlement ends. Germans enter Stalingrad.	
	9–21 Yom Kippur. Ghetto area reduced by more than half. More than 75% of population already gone. Two thousand Jewish policemen deported.

Outside Warsaw	1942	Warsaw
		9–22 SS and SD take over administration of Jewish affairs.
9–30 Hitler publicly repeats prophecy of annihilation of world Jewry.		
		10–3 First Warsaw resettlement ends.
10–10 Ordinance lists 13 ghettos and 42 Jewish quarters in the Government General.		
10–18 Jews and "Easterners" in Reich given to Gestapo by the Ministry of Justice.		
		10–20 Coordinating Committee of the resistance movement formed.
10–28 More than 50 recognized ghettos in Poland.		

Outside Warsaw	1942 Warsaw
<u>10–29</u> 16,000 Jews killed in Pinsk.	Jacob Lejkin, police officer, is shot.
<u>11–7</u> Allies land in North Africa.	
<u>11–11</u> Germany occupies Vichy France. Italy occupies Nice.	
<u>11–26</u> Russian counteroffensive begins.	
<u>11–26</u> Jewish munitions workers replaced by forced laborers from Poland.	
<u>12–4</u> Jewish fighting Organization—Zydowska Organizacja Bojowa, or Z.O.B—is founded.	
<u>12–17</u> League of Nations pledges punishment for extermination of Jewry.	

Outside Warsaw	1943	Warsaw
1943		
		January Only 40,000 Jews remain.
1–10 Ghetto uprising erupts at Minsk Mazowiecki.		
1–14 Allies agree on unconditional surrender at Casablanca meeting.		
		1–18 Second extermination begins. First resistance.
2–2 Sixth German Army surrenders at Stalingrad.		
2–5 to 2–12 First Bialystok resettlement.		
2–15 Russians take Kharkov.		
2–27 Roundup of Jewish munitions workers in Berlin for Auschwitz.		

Outside Warsaw	1943	Warsaw
March Deportation trains from Holland to Sobibor; Jews from Vienna, Prague, Luxembourg, and Macedonia are sent to Treblinka.		
3–13 Cracow Ghetto liquidated. First of new crematoria opens at Auschwitz.		
3–14 Deportations from Thrace and Salonika begin.		
		4–19 to 5–16 Liquidation: ghetto bombed, set afire, razed. Uprising in force. A concentration camp for 2,000 Jewish and Christian prisoners established on site by the SS.
August Russians advance. Lodz Ghetto survivors transferred to Auschwitz.		

Outside Warsaw	1943/1944	Warsaw
8–2 Alexander Pechersky leads insurrections at the camps in Treblinka.		
8–3 Ghetto uprising at Bedzin.		
8–16 Ghetto uprising at Bialystok.		
9–1 Tarnow Ghetto Uprising.		
10–13 Pechersky leads an insurrection at Sobibor.		
10–25 Uprising at Czestochowa Ghetto.		
11–3 Lublin Ghetto Uprising.		
1944		
		3–7 Emanuel Ringelblum executed in the ruins, together with his wife and child.

Outside Warsaw	1944/1950 Warsaw
June The Lodz Ghetto, the only remaining ghetto in Europe, is liquidated and its population is deported to Auschwitz.	
10–6 Insurrection at Auschwitz.	
1945	
1–16 Revolt at Chelmno Camp.	
5–8 War ends.	
1946	
	September Ten cases of the Ringelblum archives excavated.
1950	
	12–1 Two rubber-sealed milk cans of Ringelblum archives excavated. Documents cover history of the ghetto up to March 1943.

APPENDIX 1

Tracing Family Roots in Poland

By Fay Bussgang

Although some records of Jewish life in Poland were destroyed during the war [WWII], enough still exist to make it possible for most people with Polish-Jewish heritage to trace their roots. In this chapter, we discuss the types of documents that may be helpful in obtaining information about family members and the repositories in Poland where they can be found.

KEY RECORDS

The two most important types of records for geneological research in Poland are metrical records (*metryki*), that is, documents of birth, marriage and death; and Books of Residents (*Ksiegi Ludnosci*), population registers that contain information about all legal inhabitants of a community.

Metrical Records

From 1808–1825, births, marriages and deaths of Jews were registered in the same books with Roman Catholics; but from 1826 on, separate books were maintained for Jews (called people of the Mosaic religion—*wyznania mojzeszowego*). Metrical records less than one hundred years old can be found in local Civil Registration Offices (*Urzad Stanu Cywilnego-USC*), usually situated in the town hall. In large cities, the office may be in a separate location. However, metrical records from pre-war towns in

Eastern Galicia, once a part of Poland but now in Ukraine, are kept in a special USC office, the *Archiwum Zabuzanskie* (lands beyond the Bug River) at Ulica Jezuicka 1/3, Warsaw.

Because of the privacy laws, the public is not allowed to see metrical records that are less than one hundred years old; but if sufficient documentation is presented to show a relationship to the person whose record is being sought, the registry office will make a certified abstract of the record for a fee. A birth certificate, a letter from an official certifying the relationship, or even a family tree may be sufficient evidence to serve as proof of relationship. If one is getting a record for a friend or relative, it can be helpful if that person writes a letter on an important-looking letterhead authorizing the bearer of the letter to receive the document, and also has his/her signature guaranteed/certified by a bank or notary. If no documentation is available, sometimes the power of persuasion may achieve results.

A new law requires that all official business in Poland be carried out in the Polish language. Therefore, it is important that a Polish-speaking person accompany a visitor to the registry office if the visitor is not conversant in the Polish language.

As metrical records become more than one hundred years old, the USC in each community is required to send them to their corresponding regional state archive. Prewar metrical records for Eastern Galicia, however, are sent to the Main Archive of Old Acts (see below). All metrical records more than one hundred years old may be viewed by the public, but permission to do so must be obtained in advance from the Head Office (*Naczelna Dyrekcja*) of the State Archives in Warsaw. To get permission to use archival resources and also to find out which regional archive houses metrical records from a given town, write to Naczelna Dyrekcja Archiwow Panstwowych, Ulica Dluga 6, Box 1005, 00-950 Warsaw. Letters may be written in English, but all replies, in accordance with Polish law, will be in Polish.

It is best to notify the archives a day or two in advance of the date on which a visit is planned and what records are desired, as records must be brought from the stacks where they are stored.

To find out what metrical records have been preserved for a given town, the years covered and their present location, see Miriam Weiner's book: *Jewish Roots in Poland*, YIVO Institute, New York, 1997.

Books of Residents (Ksiegi Ludnosci) and other **Population Registers**

Books of Residents, huge bound ledgers of oversize registration sheets, are a largely untapped treasure of information for genealogical research in Poland. Unlike a census, each entry includes continuously updated information about a family, spanning a number of years. Organized by town-designated house number or, later, by street address, these books contain, in one place, the names of all members of a household, their dates and places of birth, civil status, occupation, religion, names of parents and place of previous residence. A column for notes may include date, place, and name of husband if a daughter marries; date of death if someone dies; and the new place of residence if someone moves.

From the mid-1800s until 1931, all inhabitants were required to register in the town where they had their legal residence. This was not necessarily where they actually lived. Thus, although a family may have lived in a large city, their legal residence may have been in their native village, and it is there that they would have been registered. Because of the increased mobility of people during and after WWI, these books were not always kept up-to-date. In 1932, the system of registration was modified, and residents were registered where they actually lived. From then on, all changes of address, even within the community, were noted in registration books called *Ksiegi Meldunkowe* or *Rejestry Mieszkancow*. Often utilized by the Germans during the war, these latter books survived only in certain localities.

Books of Residents and Registration Books, if they have been preserved, can be found in regional state archives and may be viewed with permission from the Head Office of the State Archives in Warsaw. Information about what books exist and where they are kept can be obtained from the Head Office.

Both metrical records and population registers were maintained principally in the Polish language. However, in Western Poland and Galicia, the German language was sometimes used, and in Central Poland, from 1868 to 1917, all official documents were written in Russian.

OTHER SOURCES

Other sources of information that may be useful for genealogical research are *kahal* (local Jewish community) and synagogue records, ghetto records, survivors' lists, notary records, business directories and address books, passport applications, community almanacs and military records. These will be listed below, with brief explanations, according to the repository in which they are located.

Jewish Historical Institute (*Zydowski Instytut Historyczny-ZIH)*

—Ulica Tlomackie 3 / 5, 00-090, Warsaw

- *Synagogue Records* (pre-war): List of members, amount of contribution to synagogue, sometimes with age and address. Available for a limited number of communities.
- *Cemeteries and Monuments*: Documentation by Jan Jagielski and Eleonora Bergman of Jewish cemeteries, synagogues and monuments in Poland.
- *Ghetto Records*: Information concerning inhabitants of ghettos in Warsaw, Bialystok, Lodz and Krakow. For Warsaw Ghetto—Ringelblum Archives (chronicle of everyday life), applications (with photos) for an identity card (*Ausweis*), and cards documenting deaths, listing date and cause of death, birth date, names of parents, address.
- *Survivors Lists*: Names of 150,000 Polish-Jewish survivors registered shortly after the war. Birth date, names of parents, address before the war, address when registered.
- *Survivors Data Base*: Data base of current information about survivors created by the Lauder Foundation's Genealogical Project at ZIH, headed by Yale Reisner.
- *Testimonies of Survivors*: Depositions taken by organizations, personal memoirs.
- *Post-War Jewish Organizations*: Records of different organizations that aided Jews after the war, including orphanages and schools. Some contain lists of names.
- *Photo Collection*: Large collection of photos, mostly uncatalogued.

For more detailed contents of ZIH archives, see Bussgang, Fay, "Archives of the Jewish Historical Institute in Warsaw," *Avtaynu*, Vol. X, No. 1, Spring 1994.

Main Archives of Old Acts *(Archiwum Glowne Akt Dawnych)*

—Ulica Dluga 7, Warsaw

- *Jewish Community Records* (*Kahal* or *Gmina Zydowska*): "CWW" collection. Documents mostly concerned with building and maintaining synagogues, collecting contributions and electing rabbis, sometimes with resolving disputes with the rabbi and/or the synagogue caretaker. When there was an election of a rabbi, all adult male synagogue members (female members, if widows) were listed indicating how they voted. Useful to genealogists in placing a person in a certain community at a given time.
- *Metrical Records from Eastern Galicia*: Records more than one hundred years old from towns now in Ukraine. Some of the oldest records, however, are still in state archives in Lviv (formerly Lwow).

Regional State Archives (*Archiwa Panstwowe*)

—Consult Head Office of Archives (*Naczelna Dyrekcja Archiwow Panstwowych*) at Ulica Dluga 6, Box 1005, 00-950 Warsaw for the correct regional archive containing records for a particular town.

- *Metrical Records and Population Registers* as noted above.
- *Notary Records:* Mostly 20th century. Each notary kept his own books, so there are several such books for a community. Prenuptial agreements, wills, distribution of property, summonses (e.g., for non-payment of rent), documentation of loans, validation of

matriculation, etc.—any kind of situation in which one might need to have an official certification that something took place.

- *Business Directories (Kalendarze)*: Published every year or so in communities like Lodz and Krakow. Much like US Yellow Pages. Contain lists of businesses, organized by trade and by location, names of owners and advertisements.
- *Address Books (Ksiegi adresowe)*: Contain lists of individuals by occupation and lists of heads of household within a city showing address and trade or profession. Sections in newer volumes may have telephone numbers, addresses of municipal offices, schools, institutions and sanitoria, as well as house owners, listed by street.
- *Applications for Identity Cards/Passports (Zaswiadczenia o tozsamosci)*: Personal data about individuals, often a photograph. Applications sometimes located in municipal archives rather than state archives.
- *Lodz State Archives*: List of ghetto inhabitants by street address, kept by German authorities. Former Lodz Residents in Tel Aviv reorganized the lists alphabetically by name. Lodz Archives, Yad Vashem and US Holocaust Memorial Museum have microfilm copies. List shows name, birth date, place of residence, all changes of places of residence, date of death if it occurred in the ghetto and date of any deportation. Yad Vashem is planning to make this list available on their website.
- *Krakow State Archives*: Applications for a German wartime identity card (*Kennkarte*) in Krakow Ghetto. Lists of property confiscated in Krakow Ghetto.

National Library (*Biblioteka Narodowa*) **AND**
—Aleje Niepodleglosci 213, Warsaw

Jagiellonian University Library (*Biblioteka Jagiellonska*)
—Aleje Mickiewicza 22, Krakow

- ➢ *Almanacs*: Almanacs of individual communities (such as Lwow, Krakow) with information on 1) Jews prominent in art, literature, music, sports, business and finance 2) political and religious life of the city, institutions of culture, charity, etc. Other almanacs specifically about Jewish literary figures, physicians, Jewish schools, Jewish healthcare organizations, Jews who fought for Poland's freedom, histories of Jews in various cities, etc.
- ➢ *Newspaper Archives*: Local press from many communities, also professional journals. Articles, obituaries (some on microfilm).

Main Medical Library (*Glowna Biblioteka Lekarska*)
—Ulica Jazdow 6, 00-476, Warsaw

- ➢ *Personal Records of Physicians and Pharmacists*: Practiced in Poland. Date of birth, training, employment, specialty, articles about or by them.

Central Military Archive (*Centralne Archiwum Wojskowe*)
—Ulica Kazimierzowska 12, 00-910 Warsaw-Rembertow

- ➢ *Military Records:* Military rank, date and place of birth, religion, names of parents (including maiden name of mother), civil status, maiden name of wife, names and ages of children, education, civil occupation, date inducted, military education, knowledge of languages, wounds, decoration and commendations. (Records for soldiers who served in the Anders Army or other Allied Armies are located in England.) It may be necessary to identify the military unit in which the person served.

TIPS FOR ADVANCE PREPARATION

1. Interview relatives. First and foremost! Find out the exact names of towns and family members, Polish spelling for towns rather than Yiddish. Be sure to get Jewish and Polish first names, not just names used in the United States.

2. On the Internet, go to website www.JewishGen.org. Search on "Family Finder" to see if anyone else is researching your family surnames. On home page, scroll down to "Hosted Organization" and click "JRI-Poland." JRI-Poland is an ambitious project of genealogists to index all Jewish metrical records for Poland. Volunteers have already indexed many towns. Do search on your surnames for towns of interest. All metrical records with that surname will be listed for you with the year and number of record and the main data contained in the document. Simplifies search for the actual (and more complete) document in Poland.

3. Consult Jewish records of birth, marriage, and death collected by the Church of Jesus Christ of Latter Day Saints (Mormons) for your Polish towns (1808–1860s). Either visit Mormon Family History Center near you, or go to Internet site: www.Ancestry.com for a list of towns for which records have been microfilmed.

4. For current Jewish institutions and activities in Poland, see Polish Jewish Community website: <http://kehillah.jewish.org.pl>.

APPENDIX 2

Practical Information

HOW TO GET THERE:

Cracow (Krakow)

Airport: Balice DRK—ten miles northwest of the city.

Warsaw

Airport: Okecie, 28 Marii Konopnickiej—six miles southwest of the city.

Airlines:

- ➢ El Al: 30-66-16/7/8
- ➢ KLM: 75-93-600
- ➢ Lot: 6-21-70-21
- ➢ Lufthansa: 89-51-277
- ➢ SwissAir: 27-50-16

BAGGAGE

The “piece” concept that prevails on transatlantic flights does not apply to intra-European or Europe-Israel flights, where the airlines can enforce 44-pound limits. Please keep this in mind when packing. If your stay in Eastern Europe is very short, lost luggage can present a considerable inconvenience. It is highly recommended that you carry toiletries, a change of undergarments, and medication in an overnight bag. Make sure luggage tags with your name and phone number are tightly affixed to your suitcase.

CLIMATE

Countrywide Average

	Jan	Feb	Mar	Apr	May	June	July	Aug	Sept	Oct	Nov	Dec
Average Low (F)	23°	24°	30°	37°	47°	51°	58°	54°	49°	40°	32°	27°
Average High (F)	32°	35°	43°	54°	67°	72°	74°	73°	65°	54°	42°	35°
Warsaw Average Rainfall (in Inches)	1	1	1	2	2	3	3	3	2	2	1	1

COMMUNICATIONS

When dialing direct to Poland, dial the proper international access code—011 from the United States—then "48" (country code), the city code, and the local number. There is a wait for overseas telephone calls in Warsaw. One way to avoid this problem is to send a telex home asking for a return call from the United States. Don't forget to give your room number.

Recently, an AT&T access number was introduced. The U.S. operator can be reached by dialing the following numbers:

WARSAW: 010-480-0111
POLAND (outside Warsaw): 0-DIAL TONE-010-480-0111

When transmitting telex messages from the United States, the code "867" must precede the telex number.

Though fax machines have recently been introduced in Poland, their reliability is often still questionable.

CURRENCY

The Polish monetary unit is the zloty, which is divided into one hundred groszy.

Coins are issued in 1, 2, 5, 10, and 20 zloty denominations, as well as in 10, 20, and 50 groszy denominations. Zloty bills are issued in the following denominations: 10, 20, 50, 100, 200, 500, 1000, and 2000. The current conversion rate is $1 US = 4.50 zloty.

ELECTRICITY

Electrical appliances run on 220 volts, at 50 cycles. A plug adapter and a converter are necessary for all electrical appliances and equipment.

EMBASSIES

- *Canada*: Ul. Matejki 1/5, 00-481, Warsaw.
  Tel: 29-80-51.
- *Great Britain*: Al. Roz 1, 00-556, Warsaw.
  Tel: 38-100-1/05 (days) and 628-100-1/02 (nights).
- *G.B. Consulate*: Ul. Wawelska 14, 02-061, Warsaw.
  Tel: 62-88-31/35.
- *Israel*: Krzywickiego 24, 02-078, Warsaw.
  Tel: 625-09-23, 625-00-28.
- *United States*: Al. Ujazdowskie 29/31, Warsaw.
  Tel: 28-30-41/9.
- *US Consulate*: Ulica Stolarska 9, 31403, Krakow.
  Tel: 22-97-64.

HOTELS

Cracow (Krakow)

- *Forum Hotel*: 28 Marii Konopnickiej. Tel: 669500. Tlx: 0322737.
- *Holiday Inn*: Ul. Koniewa 7. Tel: 375044. Tlx: 0325356.

Warsaw

- *Europejski Hotel*: Ul. Krakowskie Przedmiescie 13. Tel: 26-50-51. Tlx: 81-36-15.
- *Forum Hotel*: Nowogrodzka 24/26. Tel: 21-02-71. Tlx: 81-47-04.
- *Holiday Inn*: Ul. Zlota 2. Tel: 20-03-41. Tlx: 81-74-18, or 81-77-78.
- *Marriott*: Al. Jerozolimskie 65/79. Tel: 81-65-14. Fax: 48-22-21.
- *Victoria Intercontinental*: Ul. Krolewska 11. Tel: 27-80-11. Tlx: 81-25-16. Fax: 27-98-56.

KOSHER FOOD

There is no way to obtain kosher food in Poland, with the exception of an occasional meal at JDC-supported canteens in Cracow and Warsaw, or at the newly established Menorah restaurant in Warsaw (at Plac Grzybowski). Thus, those that are observing *kashrut* may want to bring food with them. Following are some suggested items:

- Can opener, or Swiss Army knife
- Crackers

- ➢ Flatware—one set for dairy, one set for meat
- ➢ Fruit in cans
- ➢ Granola bars, nuts, or dried fruit
- ➢ Grape juice or Wine, if "Kiddush" is desired
- ➢ Matzah in boxes, if "motzei" is desired
- ➢ Meat in vacuum-packed plastic packages
- ➢ Paper plates, napkins, and plastic sandwich bags
- ➢ Salami
- ➢ Sardines in a can
- ➢ Shabbat and Yahrzeit candles
- ➢ Tuna in cans with flip-tops

SHOPPING

Only a rather limited number of Jewish-interest items are available in Poland. At times, you will be able to find books on Jewish subjects at bookstores. The Jewish Historical Institute, on the other hand, has a considerable number of publications—mainly in Polish but also in English and Yiddish.

At tourist hotels or philatelic stores, a sterling silver coin commemorating Janusz Korczak or Ludwik Zamenhof may be available. In Cracow's Sukiennice (shopping mall), the folklore stand sells wood carvings of Hassidim.

Shopping hours are from 9 A.M. to 3 P.M. (department stores); from 6 A.M. to 6 P.M. (grocery stores); and 11 A.M. to 7 P.M. (shops). Check with the concierge for weekend hours.

TIME

Poland is six hours ahead of US Eastern Standard Time. Banking hours are from 8 A.M. to noon or 2 P.M., Monday through Saturday; while business hours run from 8 A.M. to 3 P.M.

TOBACCO AND LIQUOR

Import allowances for tobacco are one carton of cigarettes, fifty cigars, or 8¾ ounces of tobacco for travelers eighteen years of age or older. Liquor allowances are one liter for travelers seventeen or older. However, there is little need to bring tobacco or liquor into the country.

APPENDIX 3

Congregations and Synagogues

Congregation	Synagogue	House of Worship
Bielsko-Biala		
Mickiewicza 26		Mickiewicza 26
Bytom		
Smolenska 4	Pl. Grunwaldski 62	
Chrzanow		
		Chajnowska 16
Czestochowa		
Garibaldiego 18		Garibaldiego 18
Dzierzoniow		
Krasickiego 28	Krasickiego 28	
Gliwice		
Dolne Waly 9		Dolne Waly 9
Katowice		
Mlynska 13		Mlynska 13
Krakow		
Skawinska 2	Remu Szeroka 49	
	Templum Miodowa 24	
Legnica		
Chajnowska 17	Chajnowska 17	

Congregation	Synagogue	House of Worship
Lodz		
Zachodnia 78	Rewolucji 1905 r. 28	Zachodnia 78
Lublin		
Lubartowska 10		Lubartowska 10
Nowy Sacz		
		Jagielonska 12
Swidnica		
		Bohaterow Getta 22
Przyrow		
		Leloska 2
Szezecin		
Niemcewicza 2		Niemcewicza 2
Walbrzych		
Mickiewicza 18		Mickiewicza 18
Wroclaw		
Wlodkowicza 9		Wlodkowicza 9
Warszawa		
Twarda 6	Nozyka Twarda 6	
Zgorzelec		
Bohaterow Getta 3		Bohaterow Getta 3
Zary k Zagania		
Armii Czerwonej 3A	Armii Czerwonej 3A	

APPENDIX 4

Jewish Organizations

Name and Address

American Joint Distribution Committee

➢ Twarda 6
00-104 Warsaw

American-Polish Foundation for Polish-Jewish Culture

➢ Plac Grzybowski 12/16
00-950 Warsaw

American-Polish-Israeli Foundation

➢ Plac Grzybowski 6/12
00-105 Warsaw

Association of the Children of Holocaust Survivors

➢ Founded in 1991
Chairman: Jakub Gutenbaum

Folks-Sztym—Jewish Newspaper

➢ Plac Grzybowski 12/14
00-104 Warsaw

International Janusz Korczak Society

➢ Sniadeckich 17
00-654 Warsaw

Name and Address

Israeli Embassy
➢ Krzywickiego 24
25-00-28
02-078 Warsaw

Jagiellonian University—
Research Center on Jewish History and Culture in Poland
➢ Ulica Batorego 12
31-135 Cracow

The Jewish Agency
➢ Plac Grzybowski 6/12
00-104 Warsaw

Jewish Cemetery
➢ 4951 Okopowa
01-043 Warsaw

Jewish Cultural and Social Union
➢ Plac Grzybowski 12/14
00-104 Warsaw

Jewish Forum Foundation
➢ P.O. Box 129
Warsaw 13

Jewish Historical Institute
➢ 3/5 Tlomackie St.
00-090 Warsaw

Name and Address

Jewish Religious Organization
➢ Twarda 6
00-950 Warsaw

Jewish State Theater
➢ Plac Grzybowski 12/16
00-104 Warsaw

Jewish War Veterans Association

Midrash—Jewish Magazine
➢ Twarda 6
00-104 Warsaw

Nissenbaum Family Foundation
➢ Ulica Twarda 6
00-105 Warsaw

Polish Association of Righteous Gentiles
➢ c/o Int'l Janusz Korczak Society
Sniadeckow 17
00-654 Warsaw

Polish-Israeli Friendship League
➢ c/o Café Eilat
Aleje Ujazdowskie 47
Warsaw

Polish Union of Jewish Students

Name and Address

Public Committee for the Protection of Jewish Cemeteries and Endowments

> ➢ 1 Zabykami Kultury Zydowskiej W Polsce
> Ulica Piekna 44S
> 00-672 Warsaw

Ronald S. Lauder Foundation

> ➢ Twarda 6
> 00-104 Warsaw

Survivors of the Shoah Visual History

> ➢ Twarda 6
> 00-104 Warsaw

APPENDIX 5
Recommended Reading

Abramson, Samuel and Bernard Postal. *The Traveler's Guide to Jewish Landmarks of Europe*. New York: Fleet Press, 1971.

Arad, Yitzhak. *Ghetto in Flames: The Struggle and Destruction of the Jews in Vilna in the Holocaust*. New York: Yad Vashem, 1980.

Bartoszewski, Wladyslaw. *The Warsaw Ghetto: A Christian's Testimony*. Boston: Beacon Press, 1987.

Bauer, Yehuda. *The Holocaust in Historical Perspective*. Seattle: University of Washington Press, 1978.

The Chronicle of the Lodz Ghetto. Edited by Lucjan Dobroszycki. New Haven: Yale University Press, 1984.

Conot, Robert. *Justice at Nuremberg*. New York: Harper & Row, 1983.

Czerniakow, Adam. *The Warsaw Diary of Adam Czerniakow*. New York: Stein and Day, 1999.

Dawidowicz, Lucy S. *The War Against the Jews, 1933–1945*. New York: Bantam Books, 1986.

Frank, Anne. *The Diary of a Young Girl*. New York: Doubleday, 1995.

Friedlander, Albert. *Out of the Whirlwind: A Reader of Holocaust Literature*. Garden City: Doubleday, 1968.

Gilbert, Martin. *Auschwitz and the Allies*. New York: Holt, Reinhart, and Winston, 1981.

———. *The Holocaust: Maps and Photographs: A Record of the Destruction of Jewish Life in Europe during the Dark Years of Nazi Rule*. New York: Braun Center for Holocaust Studies, 1992.

———. *Holocaust Journey: Traveling in Search of the Past*. New York: Columbia University Press, 1997.

———. *Jewish History Atlas*. New York: McMillan, 1969.

———. *Never Again: A History of the Holocaust*. Universe Press.

Gutman, Israel. *The Jews of Warsaw, 1939–1943: Ghetto, Underground, Revolt*. Bloomington: Indiana University Press, 1982.

Hans Frank's Diary. Edited by Stanislaw Piotrowski. Warsaw: Panstwowe Wydawnictwo Naukowe, 1961.

Hart, Kitty. *I Am Alive*. New York: Abelard-Schuman, 1962.

Hersey, John. *The Wall*. New York: Vintage Books, 1988.

Huberband, Shimon. *Kidush Hashem: Jewish Religious and Cultural Life in Poland during the Holocaust*. New York: Yeshiva University Press, 1987.

Karski, Jan. *Story of a Secret State*. Boston: Houghton-Mifflin, 1944.

Kaufman, Michael T. *Mad Dreams, Saving Graces: Poland a Nation in Conspiracy*. New York: Random House, 1989.

Korczak, Janusz. *Ghetto Diary*. New York: Holocaust Library, 1978.

———. *King Matt the First*. New York: Farrar, Straus and Giroux, 1986.

Krajewska, Monika. *Time of Stones*. Warsaw: Interpress-Warsaw, 1983.

Krall, Hannah. *Shielding the Flame: An Intimate Conversation with Dr. Marek Edelman, the Last Surviving Leader of the Warsaw Ghetto Uprising*. New York: Henry Holt and Co., 1986

Krinsky, Carol Herselle. *Synagogues of Europe: Architecture, History, Meaning*. Cambridge: MIT Press, 1985.

Kroszczor, Henryk and Henryk Zimmler. *Cmentarz czdowski w Warszawie*. Warsaw: PWN, 1983.

Kurzman, Dan. *The Bravest Battle: The Twenty-Eight Days of the Warsaw Ghetto Uprising*. New York: Putnam, 1976.

Levi, Primo. *Moments of Reprieve*. New York: Summit Books, 1986.

Levin, Nora. *The Holocaust: The Destruction of European Jewry, 1933–1945*. New York: Schocken, 1968.

Lifton, Betty Jean. *The King of Children: A Biography of Janusz Korczak*. New York: Farrar, Straus and Giroux, 1988.

Moczarski, Kazimierz. *Conversation with an Executioner*. Englewood Cliffs: Prentice-Hall, 1981.

Notes from the Warsaw Ghetto: The Journal of Emanuel Ringelblum. Edited and translated by Jacob Sloan. New York: McGraw-Hill, 1958.

Novitch, Miriam. *Sobibor, mahaneh ha-avadon ve-ha-mered.*. Israel: Beit Lohame ha-getoat, 19(?)

Ringelblum, Emanuel. *Kronika getta warszawskiego: wrzesiean 1939—styczean 1943.*

———. *Polish-Jewish Relations during the Second World War*. Fertig, 1976.

Rings, Werner. *Life with the Enemy: Collaboration and Resistance in Hitler's Europe, 1939–1945*. Garden City: Doubleday, 1982.

Singer, Isaac Bashevis. *Magician of Lublin*. New York: Noonday Press, 1960.

Smolen, Kazimierz. *Auschwitz, 1939–1945*. Albuquerque: Route 66 Press, 1995.

Trunk, Isaiah. *Jewish Response to Nazi Persecution*. New York: Stein and Day, 1979.

Uris, Leon. *Mila 18*. Garden City: Doubleday, 1961.

Wasita, Ryszard. *In the Land We Shared*. Warsaw: Interpress-Warsaw, 1987.

Weiner, Miriam. *Jewish Roots in Poland: Pages from the Past and Archival Inventories*. New York: YIVO Institute, The Miriam Weiner Routes to Roots, Inc., 1997.

———. *Jewish Roots in Ukraine and Moldova: Pages from the Past and Archival Inventories*. New York: YIVO Institute, The Miriam Weiner Routes to Roots, Inc., 1999

Wiesel, Elie. *Night*. New York: Hill and Wong, 1960.

Wiesenthal, Simon. *Every Day Remembrance Day: A Chronicle of Jewish Martyrdom*. New York: H. Holt, 1987.

Index

Page numbers in *italics* denote illustrations

You May Also Enjoy These Other Hippocrene Titles...

Jews in Poland: A Documentary History
Iwo Cyprian Pogonowski

"Mr. Pogonowski's colorful compendium fills a very definite need . . . I learned much from reading the book. It will be a rare reader who does not do the same."

—*Professor Norman Davies, Oxford University*

A unique record of a half millennium of Polish-Jewish relations, this book describes the rise of the Jews as a nation and the crucial role in this development played by the Polish-Jewish community. The documents, many of which are made available in English for the first time, include 114 historical maps and 172 illustrations—reproductions of outstanding paintings, photographs of official posters, newspaper headlines, and political cartoons. Also included is a detailed chronicle of the Holocaust with ample annotations.

402 pages • 8 x 11 • maps/illustrations • $19.95pb • 0-7818-0604-6 • (677)

The Jewish People's Almanac, Expanded Edition
David C. Gross
Illustrated by Robert Leydenfrost

"Contains a little of everything—humor, anecdote, important historical information about the Jewish people, especially the history of Judaism in America. The period covered is vast. The main focus of the book is people, and wonderful stories abound."

—*Publisher's Weekly*

A perennial favorite, this compendium of little-known facts and illuminating insights into the history of the Jewish people is now available in an expanded edition. Long before *Schindler's List* became an Academy Award-winning film, David C. Gross recognized the importance of the story and included it among the entries in *The Jewish People's Almanac*. Also featured here are well-known Jewish-American personalities like Harpo Marx and Sammy Davis, Jr., as well as influential Jewish figures and communities worldwide.

620 pages • 6 x 9 • $19.95pb • 0-7818-0900-2 • W • (321)

Poland: An Illustrated History
Iwo Cyprian Pogonowski

"An important contribution to a better understanding of Polish history, which demonstrates in a vivid fashion the historical vicissitudes of that major European nation."

—Dr. Zbigniew Brzezinski, National Security Advisor under President Carter, and Professor of Government at Columbia University

Poland's remarkable quest for representative government, one of the oldest in modern Europe, is presented against the backdrop of a millennium of history rich in cultural, political, and social events, including centuries of Poland's civilizing role in the expansive area between the Baltic and the Black seas. These topics—complemented with Polish art, literature, music, architecture, and tradition—are described by the author in this concise volume, which also includes 50 photos, illustrations, and maps.

270 pages • 5 x 7 • 50 b/w illus. • $14.95hc • 0-7818-0757-3 • W • (404)

Poland in World War II: An Illustrated Military History
Andrew Hempel

"Any reader interested in a concise account of Polish military history in World War II should purchase a copy of this highly readable book."

—Hejnal

Poland's participation in World War II is generally little known in the West and is often reduced to stereotypes advanced by the media: of German planes attacking the civilian population in 1939 and of Polish cavalry charging German tanks. In actuality, it was not an easy victory for the Germans in 1939, and after the conquest of Poland, the Poles continued to fight in their homeland, on all European fronts, and in North Africa. This illustrated history concisely presents the Polish military war effort in WWII, intermingled with factual human interest stories and 50 black-and-white photos and illustrations.

117 pages • 5 x 7 • 50 b/w illus. • $11.95hc • 0-7818-0758-1 • W • (541)

Prices subject to change without notice. **To purchase Hippocrene Books** contact your local bookstore, call (718) 454-2366, or write to: HIPPOCRENE BOOKS, 171 Madison Avenue, New York, NY 10016. Please enclose check or money order, adding $5.00 shipping (UPS) for the first book and $.50 for each additional book.